Mindfulness with Attitude

Mindfulness with Attitude

A PRACTICAL GUIDE TO LIVING A MINDFUL LIFE

Dr Rachel Jones-Wild & Mark Sidney

MARK SIDNEY

mindful

Mindfulness Based Therapies CIC

1

Contents

Preface

In many ways this book has been around ten years in the making, perhaps longer. If we think in terms of the origins of some of the practices we are going to introduce in this book then perhaps it was 2000 years in the making, but maybe that's taking things a little far!

In 2012 I decided to train as a Breathworks mindfulness trainer. I had been meditating for some time but certainly didn't see myself as a 'natural meditator'. Rather, I was, and still am, someone who is fascinated by the human mind and how we can use psychology, and self-awareness to live happier lives. For me, meditation was a challenge, and yet I knew that the practice and philosophy of mindfulness held the key to change my life, and the lives of others.

In 2013 I founded Mindfulness Based Therapies C.I.C. (later renamed to Mindful Therapies), a social enterprise dedicated to making mindfulness available to as many people as possible in a way that was affordable and accessible. Later that year I met a strange man who wanted to find out more about mindfulness. He seemed rather cynical about the whole thing but went on to become a co-director of Mindful Therapies, co-author of this book, and one of my closest friends.

This book was also born out of the Covid19 pandemic. Some people learned languages during lockdown. Some people baked banana bread. We wrote a book! As we are finally preparing to release this book into the world I am stepping into a new chapter in my life. As I write this preface I am seven weeks away from going on maternity leave with my first child and I suspect nothing will be the same again. For the last decade Mindful Therapies has been my baby. For the last two years this book has been my baby. And now, as Mindfulness with Attitude flies the nest and makes its way in the world, I will be learning how to practice mindfulness with a real baby! I hope to put the attitudes into practice in the next chapter in my journey and I really hope that you, the reader, gain as much from reading and practising Mindfulness with Attitude as we did writing it.

Rachel Jones-Wild

The mind has always fascinated me. Since graduating with a psychology degree in 1987, I have worked in mental health addiction services and homelessness. Throughout I have explored hypnosis, NLP Positive psychology but mindfulness is where I found my place. I met Rachel in 2013 on an 8-week mindfulness course that she was delivering and the rest is history! I joined Mindful Therapies in 2014, eager to share in her vision to make the benefits of mindfulness more widespread, particularly around the North-East of England where we are based.

Over the years we have developed a range of courses based on Rachel's experience as a Breathworks mindfulness trainer and an integrative psychotherapist and my experience as a Mindfulness Association teacher and a leadership and performance coach. We have developed programmes in schools and workplaces and working with vulnerable people with a range of mental health difficulties. This book is a culmination of all that we have learned over the years. We have drawn upon some of the ideas of the mindfulness and compassion teachers who most inspire us and we have included some of the practices that we use most regularly in our own lives.

Mindfulness, and the attitudes that we discuss in this book, has changed my life. It has helped me to manage some of life's difficulties, including redundancy and chronic illness. Mindfulness meditation is training in paying attention and, when combined with a set of attitudes, it brings meaning. It has helped me find meaning in my life, I hope this book can help bring some focus and meaning to yours.

Mark Sidney

I dedicate this book to my baby daughter Matilda and my fur baby Sheema. Both have taught me more about mindfulness than any teacher ever could. I would also like to thank my mum, Sandra; stepdad, Mark; and nan, Cathy for all of their honesty, support and encouragement in all my endeavours.

Rachel

I would like to thank my wife Alison for all of her support, I would also like to thank her brother Jonathon for partly starting my mindfulness journey when he sent two mindfulness books to Alison.

I would like to dedicate this book to my two wonderful children, Lydia and Isaac

Mark

Thank you from both of us to Victoria, our colleague at Mindful Therapies, Thank you Jackie for all of your support as a board member, volunteer and friend. Thank you to our volunteers Sarah and Debbie, our trainees Davy and John and thank you to all of the people who use our services and support us every day.

Rachel and Mark

3

Introduction

Thank you for buying this book. This book is adapted from an audiobook of the same name, which was funded by the Social Enterprise Support Fund, which sought to support social enterprises that were impacted by the Covid19 pandemic. That audiobook was, in turn, adapted from the Mindful Therapies Getting Started Programme, which we have delivered as a 10-week rolling programme, both online and offline, in various settings, for a number of years. This book has been on quite a journey!

This book is suitable for absolute beginners as well as those with some previous experience of mindfulness. It is divided into lessons rather than chapters with the view that it can be read and used as a course. In this course, therefore, you will learn some definitions of mindfulness and we will also dispel some of the myths around what mindfulness isn't. The course includes short bitesize meditations as well as longer practices and each lesson will focus on a different attitude of mindfulness and how we can apply this attitude to our mindfulness practice as well as our everyday lives.

About Us

Rachel

I discovered meditation in the late 1990s when I was a teenager. I had fallen out with my friends at school and was searching for something. I found a class in my local library and went along, not really knowing what to expect. Meditation helped me to pause and learn to get to know myself at a time when life seemed really confusing. In 2006 I discovered Buddhism and became heavily involved in my local Buddhist Centre. This gave my life a sense of structure and meaning. The more I learned about meditation and the psychological elements of Buddhism, the more resilient I became and the richer my life became. I realised that I wanted to share what I had learned with others. I started leading meditations in 2007 and then trained as a secular mindfulness teacher in 2013. I no longer identify as a Buddhist and now practice mindfulness in a secular context.

I am now a psychotherapist and mindfulness informs my work with clients. It helps me to be more present with the other person and I regularly use mindfulness techniques to help psychotherapy clients manage their immediate symptoms.

It was the Dharma (teachings) that I most valued about Buddhism. Today it is the psychological aspects of mindfulness and the foundational attitudes that provide a framework for my life. I am really excited to be able to create this book that focuses on the foundational attitudes of mindfulness. For me these attitudes are attitudes for life.

Mark

I was first taught to meditate at school in 1980, although at the time I didn't actually know it was meditation! One of the teachers would sometimes ask us to focus on our breath or physical sensations. I found it calming and used the technique from time to time when feeling stressed. I went off to university and nobody else seemed to do it - certainly no one talked about it. So for the next thirty years I was an occasional secretive meditator. I worked for most of those 30 years in homelessness and addiction services and found that meditation helped manage my stress and, in particular, maintain a separation between my work and home life. I was made redundant in 2010 and became aware of this thing called mindfulness. It brought context and meaning to my previously irregular and unstructured practice. However, it was not until I experienced redundancy for a second time in 2012 that my practice became consistent and regular. In 2013 I completed an 8-week Breathworks mindfulness course: I became fascinated by the science; I embraced the attitudes; it felt like coming home. In 2015 I suffered a period of illness and was diagnosed with a chronic pain condition. A life-threatening allergic reaction to the medication means I now rely solely on mindfulness and meditation to manage my condition.

In 2016 I trained as a mindfulness teacher to bring the benefits I have received from practicing mindfulness to others.

The Foundational Attitudes of Mindfulness

The nine attitudes that we'll be focusing on in this book were identified by Jon Kabat Zinn when he developed the Mindfulness Based Stress Reduction programme. We can apply these attitudes to our mindfulness practice and to our everyday lives.

The nine attitudes are:

- beginner's mind;
- non-judgement;
- gratitude;
- acceptance;
- non-striving;
- letting go;
- generosity;
- patience; and
- trust.

Mindfulness involves bringing this set of attitudes to our experience. Underpinning all of these attitudes is a kindly curiosity about what is happening, when it is happening. We are taking a step back and observing what's going on. Scientific research shows that mindfulness is effective in boosting focus, productivity and connection whilst reducing stress and overwhelm. Regular practice has been shown to help manage symptoms of depression, anxiety, and chronic pain as well as increasing levels of happiness.

There are three elements to mindfulness:

Intention - to purposefully be present

Attention – practicing being aware in the present

Attitude – How we respond to what we become aware of in the present

How to Use This Book

The book is divided into nine lessons. We suggest that you read one lesson per week. You may choose to re-read the lesson during the week but try to avoid reading ahead! We know it might be tempting! Instead, spend the time between lessons reflecting on what you have learned and practising that week's meditations.

Each lesson will cover a different aspect of Mindfulness and will include:

1. information about one of the foundational attitudes of mindfulness
2. the science which backs it up and how it applies to our lives.
3. guided mindfulness practices - these form the backbone of each session
4. suggestions and tips for practising in the context of our daily lives, including home practice exercises.

In each lesson there will be a story or reflection from Mark or Rachel's personal experience. This will be written in italics.

- Guided meditations will be bullet pointed.
- Guided audio meditations are available via registration on the Mindful Therapies website mindfultherapies.org.uk/register

To get the most from this course you might find it helpful to get yourself a notebook or journal so that you can write down any reflections you may have.

Acknowledgements

We are all inspired by different people and schools of thought. This book is co-created by Rachel and Mark and, as such the acknowledgements reflect two different but overlapping journeys. The list is not exhaustive as we both owe a debt of gratitude to many practitioners and teachers in mindfulness. When we teach mindfulness courses, we often say at the outset that we are not experts. Rather, we are all experts of our own experience. We say this to encourage participants to share their experiences during the class. But we also say it because it is true. We are also grateful to every participant on every version of every course that we have taught. Their insights have helped to shape the courses that we teach and have helped to shape this book.

Rachel's Acknowledgements

I trained with Breathworks between 2010 and 2013. Breathworks was established by Vidyamala Burch and the programme was first developed to help participants to manage chronic pain and illness. In time, they also developed a course for stress. Vidyamala has written several books including Living Well with Pain and Illness published in 2008 and Mindfulness for Health, co-written with Danny Penman published in 2013. This course is partly inspired by the learning I gained from my Breathworks training.

This course also draws upon the work of Kristin Neff. The compassionate acceptance practice in lesson four is adapted from a meditation by Kristin Neff. Her book, 'Self-Compassion' published in 2011 outlines the definition of self-compassion that she found in her research and provides valuable tools for developing greater compassion towards ourselves. I also use Kristin Neff's work in my work as a psychotherapist and in my work as a trainer for counsellors.

This course is partly structured around the foundational attitudes of mindfulness as devised by Jon Kabat-Zinn. Jon Kabat-Zinn is credited as being one of the founding fathers of secular mindfulness, bringing the teachings of mindfulness to the West in the 1970s. This course would not exist without the work of Jon Kabat-Zinn. Jon Kabat-Zinn has written a number of books. We would particularly recommend the revised edition of *Full Catastrophe Living*, published in 2013 and *Wherever you go, there you are* published in 2004. As I stated above, I feel that the attitudes of mindfulness are attitudes for life and, even in times when I find meditation practice difficult (more on that later), the attitudes inform my life.

Mark's Acknowledgements

As previously mentioned, I was first taught to meditate at school, and I would like to thank John Constidine for providing the foundation for my future learning. My first structured training was the 8-week Breathworks Mindfulness for Stress course, which I attended in 2013. Under the guidance of Rachel Jones-

Wild I learned the fundamental principles of mindfulness. My training as a teacher started with the Mindfulness Association in 2015. The Mindfulness Association's Mindfulness Based Living Programme has influenced the content and practices contained within this book. Additionally, I trained as a teacher to deliver WorkplaceMT with the Mindfulness Exchange. This workplace focused programme is based on Mindfulness Based Cognitive Therapy (MBCT) as developed by Mark Williams. A practical introduction to MBCT can be found in the book *Finding Peace in Frantic World* by Mark Williams and Danny Penman (2011).

The model of the emotional regulation system discussed in this course was developed by Paul Gilbert and introduced in his book *The Compassionate Mind* 2009. This course also incorporates concepts and approaches to manage the emotional regulation system developed by Rick Hanson in his book *Hardwiring Happiness* (2013).

4

Setting an intention

Intention is:

'A deep, sincere desire, underpinned by a belief that it is possible.'

Juliet Adams, Intention Matters, 2020

An intention is a guiding principle for how you want to be and is a way of imagining a positive future self for ourselves. Before embarking on a programme of mindfulness, it is important to ask yourself why you have decided to do this course and what you hope to gain from it. This can help you to stay focused and motivated. You might ask yourself what matters most to you and use your answer to keep yourself focused and motivated.

What is the difference between a goal and an intention?

People often get confused about the difference between a goal and an intention. One of the key differences is that a goal is very specific - it has a clear end point. Whereas an intention is a direction of travel. Also, goals are often externally generated;

they are chosen by others or chosen based on the expectations of others. For example, we might set ourselves a goal to give up smoking. This might be at least in part because of pressure from others, telling us to 'kick the habit.' An intention, however, is internally generated; it is how we want to be, based on our values, our beliefs and our desires. For example, we might set an intention to live a healthier lifestyle - and this might lead us to reduce or stop smoking.

In the above example, stopping smoking as a goal is very specific; failure to achieve this goal could potentially lead to frustration and self-criticism, Whereas, setting an intention to live a healthier lifestyle could well lead to a change in smoking behaviour - but also behaviour changes in other aspects of our lives.

Additionally, goals are often expected to be realistic. Intentions, however can enable us to achieve things we would not have thought possible. Intention gives us the opportunity to unleash our creativity and imagination!

Intention setting meditation

The first meditation that we will introduce in this course is an intention setting practice. It is effectively a guided reflection in which you are invited to pause, ground yourself, and reflect on a series of questions. We would suggest that you write down anything that emerges from the reflections in your journal. You might choose to simply set an intention at the beginning of the course and refer back to it at the end. However, regular intention-setting can be incredibly helpful. You might choose to use this practice every Monday morning to set your intention for the week. Or you might choose to set an intention at the beginning of every period of meditation to help you to stay focused.

Before beginning the meditation itself, you can use your meditation posture to set your intention. Our posture in meditation indicates to our body and mind that we are about to meditate. This does not mean we have to sit in the lotus position with our hands resting on our knees and thumbs touching our middle fingers as is often depicted. If this is comfortable for you then great. Although we do not need to follow an externally defined posture, it is important to find a posture that works for you. The important thing is to find a comfortable posture of relaxed alertness that indicates your intention to meditate. Ideally the back should be upright and if comfortable supporting itself. Not too rigid but not slouching. We suggest that your hands should be open and relaxed resting on the lap or by your side. If sitting on a chair, then we suggest that both feet should be flat on the floor. Your eyes can either be closed or you may choose to soften the focus on a neutral point in front of you. We suggest that your head should be in a neutral position supported by the neck, neither gazing up nor down.

- Find yourself a comfortable meditation posture (see above). Lightly close your eyes if that feels comfortable for you.
- Bring your attention to a sense of being grounded. You might do this by observing the felt sensations of the feet on the floor and the contact you can feel with your chair. You might also ground yourself by taking a few deep breaths.

- You might take a few moments to scan the body for any signs of tension. When you notice tension, see if you can let it go.
- When you are ready, ask yourself the following questions, giving yourself a couple of minutes to reflect on each:

1. What matters to me right now?
2. Why did I buy this book?
3. How would I like to be by the end of this course?

- There are no right or wrong answers. Just notice anything that emerges when you ask the questions.
- When you are ready, let go of the questions and return your attention to your breath.
- Bring the meditation to a close in your own time and open your eyes.

5

lesson one: beginner's mind

Welcome to lesson one. In this lesson we begin by dispelling some of the myths around mindfulness. Mindfulness is not a relaxation practice. Nor does it aim to empty the mind. And while mindfulness can help a whole range of people to manage a whole range of difficulties, it is not a panacea. And it is not a religious practice. As such it is suitable for people of all faiths and those with no faith at all.

The first attitude we explore is beginner's mind. This is the attitude of experiencing the world as though for the very first time. And it is practised through everyday mindfulness. In this lesson we will practice mindful coffee drinking, but you can adapt this practice to any ordinary activity.

This week's main meditation is a settling and grounding practice. Perfect for managing the unsettled mind.

What Mindfulness Isn't

You may have already practised a little mindfulness before. Perhaps you have downloaded an app or been to an introductory session. Maybe you have an idea of what mindfulness is, or maybe it is completely new. Mindfulness has become increasingly popular over the last few decades and while this is largely positive, the wealth of mindfulness 'products' available means that there is some confusion and misconception about what mindfulness is and what it isn't. For example, no bookshop would be complete without a section of mindfulness colouring books. Colouring in is not mindfulness! It is possible to bring some of the principles of mindfulness to the activity of colouring in – but the activity is not mindful in and of itself.

The following misconceptions are also common:

1. *'Mindfulness should be relaxing.'* – One of the most common misconceptions is the idea that mindfulness meditation is a relaxation practice. This means that those who meditate and do not feel relaxed feel that they are doing it wrong. Alternatively, those who do feel relaxed might have a pleasant experience, but they might miss the point of why mindfulness can be so helpful. Relaxation is a pleasant by-product for some people but is not the aim. The aim is to simply become aware.

2. *'I can't practice mindfulness because I am religious'/ 'I can't practice mindfulness because I am not religious.'* Many of the practices that we learn in mindfulness courses come from Buddhist practices, However, they are completely secular. They can be practised by people of any faith or those with

no faith at all. In fact, there is a tradition of meditation within most major religions including Christianity and Islam. However, we cannot speak for every faith. While we believe that a mindfulness practice of becoming aware of what is happening in the present moment could be compatible with most faiths, we respect that this might not be right for everyone.

3. *'Mindfulness is easy'* – This myth definitely comes from someone who hasn't tried it! Although the practices may appear simple, we are conditioned to always be doing something - mindfulness is the process of non-doing, of just being and observing without judgement. It is a skill and as with any skill the more you practice the stronger it gets.

4. *'Mindfulness is too hard! I can't do it right.'* There is no right or wrong way to feel when we practice meditation and mindfulness, and you might not experience the outcome you expect every time. You might find yourself becoming distracted, uncomfortable or irritated and while this might not be what you wanted to experience, it doesn't mean you are doing it all. It is all data! Everything you experience is giving you information. There are also many different ways to practice so your mindfulness practice might look different to someone else's and that is absolutely fine. Having said that, mindfulness is a practice. Mindfulness is a natural human trait, we all have the innate ability to be mindful, but it is also a skill that can be developed by applying certain principles, techniques and attitudes. Swimming is also an innate human ability

- we can all stay afloat in water and progress through it, however, being able to swim effectively requires the application of strokes. Our physical posture and movements whilst in the water directly affect how successful we will be in staying afloat and progressing. Likewise with mindfulness our posture and the attitude (mental strokes) we bring to our sea of thoughts will affect whether we stay afloat and progress.

5. *'Mindfulness can solve everything!'* - There are many claims and scientific studies demonstrating a massive list of benefits of mindfulness practice. These benefits are possible and may be achieved. However, they require many hours of practice. When we practice, we are not trying to make anything happen, we are just noticing what is happening in the present moment.

Before discussing the next three myths we would like to invite you to take part in two short exercises to demonstrate how the mind works.

For the first exercise we would like you to please close your eyes and bring to mind a white door and for the next few moments try to maintain your focus just on this white door.

In all likelihood your mind will have wandered off either to something related to the door or something apparently unrelated, and research suggest that this will have happened within 5-8 seconds. The door will have been familiar, it will have been based on a door you have seen before and therefore based on past experience. You may have made judgements about the colour, shape or size of the door. You may have wondered what was on the other side of the door. You may have decided whether it was an internal or external door and what sort of building it was part of. Your mind will have tried to make sense of the door. However, your mind may also have wandered to something else altogether. The mind is constantly processing stimuli and random thoughts naturally arise.

It is natural for the mind to wander. For the next exercise, we would again like you to close your eyes, but this time allow the mind to wander freely, except for the next few moments please do not think about a white door. So what does this tell us about our minds? And what does this tell us about mindfulness?

Research would suggest that you probably couldn't help thinking about the white door, and the more you tried to block it out the more persistent it became. Again this is perfectly natural, the more we try to block something the stronger it gets, instead, in mindfulness we acknowledge it is there and allow it to be there with a kindly acceptance.

6. *'I can't do mindfulness because I have too many thoughts. I can't empty my mind!'* It is virtually impossible to empty our minds of thoughts, and this is not what we are trying to do. Instead, we are trying to become more aware of our thoughts and respond to them more intentionally.

7. *'I can't do mindfulness because my mind keeps wandering.'*
   - The mind wanders, in fact mind wandering increases efficiency of the mind, encourages rest and facilitates creativity. Mindfulness meditation is not about stopping the

mind from wandering, it is about noticing where it has wandered to and choosing our response.

8. *'My meditation was bad because I couldn't block out the thoughts/ sounds/ emotions!'* Mindfulness isn't blocking negative thoughts or unpleasant emotions - The mind is less effective when dealing with negative action statements compared to positive affirmations. Energy follows focus, so when we try to block out a thought or emotion, we are actually focusing on the thing that we don't want to do and therefore giving it energy.

Now we have dispelled some of the myths and misconceptions of mindfulness, we can start to explore and discover what mindfulness is. We develop our awareness through not-knowing. By letting go of any preconceived ideas we can open up to learning with a beginner's mind.

Beginners Mind

In the beginner's mind there are many possibilities, but in the expert's there are few. **Shunryu Suzuki, Zen Mind: Beginner's Mind**

The "beginner's mind" is a mind that is willing to see everything as if for the very first time. It allows us to look beyond expectations based on past experiences, and to be receptive to new possibilities. Children naturally experience the world in this way. Because everything is new, children can be so much more curious and often ask incredibly insightful questions about the world around them. We can learn so much from children. Or perhaps it is a case of unlearning the expertise we have developed as adults!

Our minds can be lazy. When we become familiar with something we often stop paying attention. We assume that we know what something is because we have experienced something similar before, so we stop appreciating and experiencing fully.

This can mean that we continue with the same tried and tested habits and behaviours rather than finding new ways of responding and problem-solving. We just react automatically to whatever life throws at us, with the risk of making the same mistakes! What would happen if we looked at a challenge at with beginner's mind?

Why not be a tourist in your own city? When we travel, we look around us. And yet when we are at home we ignore the beauty of our own city because it is ordinary. When we look with beginner's mind, we can see our home through the eyes of a tourist. We might notice something we have never seen before!

In relationships, the closer we are to someone, the less we actually see them. We stop looking and rely on assumptions. People can be full of surprises when we see them with beginner's mind! Next time you see a colleague or loved one, see what happens if you let go of the assumptions and approach them with beginner's mind.

We might practice beginner's mind by carrying out an ordinary activity more mindfully. Rather than acting on autopilot, we bring all our senses into the experience.

Everyday Mindfulness: Making the Most of Your Coffee Break

How often do you make yourself a cup of tea or coffee and then get distracted, so it goes cold? Or maybe you really look forward to your cuppa and then by the time you get to drink it you are too stressed, or too busy multi-tasking to really enjoy it? Your drink of choice can be an opportunity to be mindful. This might be a luxurious 20-minute meditative coffee-break, or it might be just a couple of sips taken with full awareness.

When we drink a cup of coffee mindfully, we step out autopilot. When we are on autopilot, we are doing one thing whilst thinking about something else. This is completely normal and some of the time can help us to be more efficient. However, it can also lead to mistakes - such as taking a wrong turn when driving somewhere new because our autopilot is taking us down a familiar route. Autopilot also means that we miss out on experiencing our lives - and our coffee - to the fullest.

When practising a mindful activity, what is important is the level of awareness that we bring to the experience. The following description assumes that you are drinking a cup of coffee, but you can adapt the instructions for the beverage of your choice:

- When waiting for the kettle to boil, notice your own body. If you are standing, notice your feet on the ground. Notice if you are holding any tension. Take the opportunity to soften tension and take a breath.

- Use your senses in the preparation of your drink. Notice

the steam rising from the kettle. Notice the sound of the water as it boils.

- You might observe the many simple movements that you make when making your drink: bending down to take the milk from the fridge; adding your sugar....

- When you get to drink your drink, why not make it a full sensory experience?

- Firstly make sure that you are not going to be distracted by your phone, TV or other device and find a comfortable place to sit with your coffee. Notice how it feels to be sitting.

- Next, notice what you can see. Notice the colour and design of the mug. Notice the colour of the liquid. Notice the steam rising from the mug.

- Notice what you can feel. Notice the temperature of the mug. You might also notice if the mug is completely smooth or whether there are any bumps or ridges.

- Notice the smell of your drink. And notice what happens as you smell your drink. Does it make your mouth water? Does it make you feel impatient to take the first sip?

- Take a sip. Notice how the liquid feels in your mouth. Notice the flavour of your drink. Notice how it feels as you swallow. Notice any sounds.

- If you notice your mind wandering, not to worry. This is normal! Just congratulate yourself for noticing and bring your attention back to the present moment and back to your cuppa.

Rachel's Story: Everyday Mindfulness

I am a notoriously busy person. And I am often accused of being untidy. This is often because I cram my day full of lots of different tasks and I don't always give myself the time to tidy up one task before beginning the next one. This is also true of my laptop - I often have several different programmes running at once meaning that everything runs far slower than it should do.

For me everyday mindfulness means making the time to make

time. By carving out five minutes to shut down my laptop properly at the end of my working day I find that my laptop runs more efficiently, and I save time. By tidying up my papers and books and whatever else I have been using as I go along, I save myself the mammoth task of sorting my entire office in one sitting!

Everyday mindfulness means making an ordinary activity into an act of self-care rather than a chore. For example, taking five minutes in the morning to mindfully make my bed is both a mindful activity in the present moment and an act of self-care towards my future self. And when I get into a lovely made bed at the end of the day I sleep better and am more alert and focused the next day.

For me, practising these simple everyday mindful activities means breaking the habit of multi-tasking - or at least loosening the habit. And learning to enjoy tasks one moment at a time.

The Unsettled Mind

Our untrained minds are generally very busy places, and rarely settled. In any given moment our brain is processing thousands of pieces of information, taking in information from our senses, cataloguing and storing information from previous moments and planning and fantasising about the next moments. Our unsettled minds can be lost in the past, fantasising about the future or analysing and questioning the present. It can be here, or it can be off in a distant land. The unsettled mind is random and unpredictable; thoughts pop in without invitation and we feel the need to do something with them. We have no control over which thoughts arise or our immediate emotional responses and our minds continually flit from one thing to the next. The first part of mindfulness training is to recognise the unsettled mind and take back some control. Often likened to training a puppy, we patiently train the mind to settle. As we would with a puppy we gently bring the mind back to where we want it to be with kindness and patience, over and over again. We start our training with the settling and grounding practice.

Settling and Grounding Meditation

- Find a comfortable relaxed meditation position of your choice, letting go of any sense of holding.

- When you are ready, gently turn your attention to the breath. Notice what it feels like to breathe. Notice what it feels like to breathe in and notice what it feels like to breathe out.

- Now, without straining or forcing, allow the breath to deepen and lengthen slightly. Try to keep the in-breath and out-breath of equal length. You might find it useful to count to three or four on the in-breath and the same on the out-breath.

- You may find it helpful to use phrases. Say to yourself 'I am breathing in' as you breathe in and 'I am breathing out' as you breathe out.'

- This means that you are doing two things – noticing the felt sensations of each breath and gently regulating and equalising the breath with counting or a phrase. Spend a few minutes regulating the breath in this way.

- Before long you will notice that your mind has wandered. That's ok, that's what our minds do. We are not trying to stop or block out our thoughts. Instead, we are choosing not to get involved, gently returning our attention to the breath and the counting or phrase each time. Similarly, if you become distracted by sounds or physical sensations, just notice and again return to the breath and counting.

- Now allow a little bit more of your attention to rest on the out-breath, noticing the physical sensations as the body releases the breath. You may notice how the body naturally softens and relaxes as you breathe out.

- The mind can learn from the body. The body releases the breath, and the body relaxes, the mind releases involvement with thinking and the mind can begin to settle.

- Now, letting go of the counting or phrase and allowing the body to breathe itself, turn your attention to the contact with the surfaces supporting you.

- Notice the gentle pull of gravity on the soles of the feet, the sensations of pressure from the weight of the body resting on the ground or chair. Open up to the sense of touch and allow a sense of being held and supported unconditionally by the ground beneath you.

- No need to make any effort, nothing to do, nowhere to

go, just being. Mind resting in the body, body resting on the ground.

- When you are ready, open up to the space around you. Notice the temperature in the room and any sounds inside or outside the room before bringing the practice to a close.

Lesson One: Summary

Mindfulness is not a relaxation practice. Mindfulness does not require you to empty your mind. Instead, mindfulness is a practice of becoming aware of what is happening in the present moment.

When we practice with beginner's mind, we let go of expertise and observe the world as though for the very first time. When we carry out an ordinary activity mindfully, we step out of autopilot and experience that activity with full awareness, and a sense of beginner's mind.

It is normal for the mind to be unsettled. Mindfulness practice is a form of brain training that enables the mind to settle.

Lesson One Home Practice

This week see if you can find some everyday activities to carry out more mindfully. We suggest that you carry out one mindful activity each day. You might choose the same task each day or you might choose to explore a range of activities. By choosing the same task throughout the week and bringing a sense of beginner's mind, you may find that you notice different things each time. You might choose to take a mindful shower, noticing the fragrance of your shower gel and the feel of the water on your skin. Or you might choose to clean your teeth mindfully, take a mindful walk, or even wash the dishes mindfully. Make a note in your journal of your observations.

Practice the settling and grounding meditation each day. You might try this meditation at different times during the day. You might notice that your experience is different in the morning compared with the afternoon or evening. Make a note of anything you notice in your journal.

Questions for Reflection

Q1. Now that you have completed lesson one, how would you define mindfulness?

Q2. What happens when you step out of autopilot and experience beginner's mind?

6

lesson two: non-judgement

Welcome to lesson two. In this lesson we begin by exploring how to establish a mindfulness practice. Developing a new habit can be challenging at first so it is important to celebrate when we do practice rather than criticise ourselves when we don't.

This week's attitude is non-judgement. While judgement is a normal part of human experience, mindful meditation can help us to practice loosening our judgements and simply observing our experience.

This week we also consider the importance of body awareness. When we become aware of the body, we can be more present, and we can gain valuable information about our emotions enabling us to make positive choices. It is easy for us to spend so much time in our heads that we can feel disconnected from our body. Bringing our awareness to our bodily sensations (interoception) and to posture and movement (proprioception) can help us to reconnect and bring a oneness to body and mind.

We will introduce two practices. Firstly, we introduce the body scan meditation, which is an opportunity to tune into the body in a non-judgemental and kindly way. Secondly, we introduce the practice of mindful movement, an opportunity to bring stillness to the mind through focusing on the sensations of bodily movement

Home Practice Review: Starting a Mindfulness Practice

You have now been practising mindfulness for a week. And hopefully you have begun to journal about your experiences. We suggested that you meditate every day. If you did then that's great. However, if you missed a day, how did that feel? We have a tendency to criticise ourselves if we don't do what we set out to do. So perhaps you intended to meditate every day and instead you meditated four times. Or perhaps you forgot all about the everyday mindfulness activity and tried to fit in seven activities today! Instead of criticising yourself for the days that you missed, what would it be like if you celebrated the days when you remembered? What would it be like to bring a sense of non-judgement into your mindfulness practice?

Starting a mindfulness practice means starting a new habit. This takes time. And because meditation takes some effort, it can be tempting to put it off. This is all normal! However, when we criticise ourselves, we wind up feeling like failures and this makes us less likely to commit to a positive change.

Non-Judgement

The ability to observe without evaluating is the highest form of intelligence.

Jiddu Krishnamurti

We are constantly generating judgments about our experience. Everything we see is labelled and categorised. This is normal. We are not usually aware of it and we don't need to stop it altogether. However, we can become aware of it, and choose not to buy into it. When we become aware of this constant stream of judging and step back from it, then we can see through our prejudices and fears to find alternative solutions.

The mind automatically filters stimuli and experiences into one of three categories:

1. **Good** – I like this, I want more of this, hold onto it, I want this to last;
2. **Bad** – I don't like this, I want this to stop, I want to block this, push it away or pretend it's not there;
3. **Neutral** – Not relevant, not important, no need to waste time or energy on this, just ignore it.

This is perfectly natural, perfectly human, it is what our mind does. Much of the time these judgements are helpful, they can keep you safe, they can inform decisions to achieve goals, and identify possible new friendships and connections. However, these judgements are often based on old data. They are based on our past experiences - things we have been told, and things we have read or heard. This old data is not necessarily factual or relevant to the current situation. If reacted to automatically it can close us off from experiences and opportunities. By going along with judgements automatically we start developing habitual patterns of behaviour. Sometimes these habitual behaviours lead to us continuing with something we originally judged as good that now no longer serves us well, or habitually avoiding situations we have judged as bad even though circumstances are different. By ignoring the neutral we are cutting ourselves off from new experiences.

Additionally, all this judging and reacting is energy intensive. Judgements lead to us doing something, chasing and grasping the good, pushing away or turning from the bad and ignoring the seemingly irrelevant. These judgements effect every area of our lives.

We are often our own worst critic and our tendency to judge ourselves can lead us to second guessing and self-doubt. If we can suspend self-judgement, we can often be more decisive. We often judge others when we don't need to. This might apply to our colleagues, friends, loved ones or even strangers. And we tend to judge without knowing the full information. Suspending judgement can lead to more harmonious relationships.

We often judge our meditation practice because we don't feel how we want to or how we think we should feel. This can get in the way of our practice. In mindfulness we simply notice how things are. Mindfulness is about non-doing and when we practice non-judgement, we accept the present moment as it is without the need to hold on, push away or ignore anything that arises. It means opening up to our full experience. We simply allow the data to be there without analysing it.

Practicing non-judgement doesn't mean not making judgements. That's just not how our minds work. Instead, it is noticing the judgement and letting it go without reacting or judging ourselves for the judgement!

Why Body Awareness is Important

This lesson we will be introducing the body scan meditation and the practice of mindful movement. This is an opportunity to become aware of felt sensations in the body. Often, we ignore our bodies and spend much of our time stuck in our heads, focusing only on our thoughts - often about the past or the future. However, body awareness is important for a number of reasons:

1. **Releasing tension.** We often hold tension in our bodies when we are feeling stressed or when we have been sitting or standing in a particular position that is unhelpful to us. If we do not know that tension is there then we can continue to hold it until it causes problems such as strain and pain in the back, neck, and shoulders. When we become aware, we have a choice to let go and release tension or change posture, reducing the likelihood of such pain developing.

2. **Awareness of emotions.** There is a link between our bodily sensations, our emotions, our thoughts, and our actions. When we feel strong emotions we may experience a change in heart rate, tension, a change in temperature or a myriad of other 'symptoms.' Again, this is

something we may overlook. By becoming aware of our bodily sensations, we can become aware of our emotions and start to understand why we feel the way we feel. Perhaps something has irritated us, or we are worried about something that is outside of our awareness. If we are unaware of how we feel we might find ourselves becoming irritable and snapping at someone or distracting ourselves from our feelings in other ways. If we become aware of our emotions, through our physical cues, we can choose to respond more appropriately and more mindfully.

3. **The body tells us what it needs.** When we become aware of sensations in the body it becomes easier to practice self-care. For example, we might pause and notice that we feel tired and suddenly realise that we have been sleeping less than usual. This awareness enables us to make choices about our sleep habits. Body awareness is also particularly important around food and nutrition. We often eat out of habit, and we stop eating when we have cleared our plate. However, our bodies can tell us when we are hungry and how much food we *actually* need. By learning to tune into our bodies we can start to notice what we need.

4. **The body is an anchor**. We spend much of our time focusing our thoughts on the past and the future. This can often mean that we are dwelling on past mistakes and misfortunes or worrying about something that may or may not happen in the future. When we focus on felt sensations in the body, we become aware of the present moment. This can help us to calm our minds.

5. **The body is amazing!** When we are not ignoring our bodies, we are often critical. We notice the aspects of our bodies that don't look as we would like, or feel as we would like, or do what we would like them to do. By practising mindful awareness of the body, we can start to appreciate our amazing human bodies - imperfect as they may be - for all that they can do.

Everyday Mindful Activity: Introduction to Mindful Movement

Mindful movement involves focusing our awareness to notice physical and mental sensations as we move. As such it reinforces the mind body connection. Movement is the embodiment of mindfulness. Ultimately, all meditation involves implicitly paying attention to movement - sensations of the breath as it moves through the body, awareness of thoughts as they arise in the mind, changing vibrations that we call sound. With movement meditation we explicitly pay attention to the sensations of each movement. Any movement can be approached mindfully, and mindful movement can be practiced informally and as a more formal meditation.

If we can pay attention to our moving body, detecting subtle differences and changes, we can gradually learn to detect these subtle patterns in our minds also. It may seem obvious, but our minds and body are part of a connected whole and the relationship between both is symbiotic. Our bodies can learn from and react to our minds, but equally these relationships work both ways. Our body reflects our internal experience as much as our minds respond to our physical experiences.

The principles of mindful movement are the same as all mindfulness practices – To pay attention, on purpose and without judgement to what is occurring in each moment.

Examples of Mindful Movement

In the following exercises only do what feels right for your body. Remember, you are the expert when it comes to knowing your own body, if it starts to feel uncomfortable or painful - stop.

In the following examples of mindful movement that we can practice at any time, notice what happens to your thoughts when you align movement with the ebb and flow of your breath.

Lotus Flower Hands

- Starting with either your right or left hand, open your hand fully with fingers wide and spread apart. Notice your breathing.
- With the next out-breath slowly bring the tips of your fingers and thumb together.
- As you breathe in, slowly open the hand and fingers again
- Repeat in time with the breath, just allowing the movement to follow the natural ebb and flow of your breath, so you don't need to think about the movement, allowing your attention to rest on the raw physical sensations of the movement.
- Breathing in – opening;
- Breathing out – closing;
- Notice sensations in the fingers, the back of the hand the

palm, the forearm, and anywhere else where you can feel the effect of movement.

- You might notice how this feels with your eyes closed and with your eyes open.
- Repeat for ten breaths.
- Before repeating with the other hand take a moment to hold both hands out and explore any differences between the hand that has been moving and the hand that has been still. There is no right or wrong way to feel, just notice your experience right now.
- Repeat with the other hand.

Lifting and Lowering the Arms

- Either sitting or standing, allow the arms to hang loosely by your side.
- Take a few moments to notice the contact between your body and the surfaces supporting you. If you are standing, notice your feet on the ground. If you are sitting, notice your feet on the ground and your bottom on the chair or ground.
- Turn your attention to the breath. Breathing in, you are aware that you are breathing in. Breathing out, you are aware that you are breathing out. Rest your attention on the breath, gently allowing the breath to deepen and lengthen. Take three breaths in this way.
- On the next in-breath slowly bring your arms up to the sides to shoulder height in time with the in-breath.

- As you breath out allow the arms to fall back to the sides of your body.
- Allow this movement to follow the natural ebb and flow of your breath. Rising with the in-breath. Falling with the out-breath.
- Gently direct the spotlight of your attention to the felt sensations of the movement. What does it feel like to move your arms in this way?

Walking Meditation

Another way to practice mindful movement is through walking meditation. When we practice walking meditation, the intention is just to walk! With nowhere to go, no destination in mind, no purpose other than exploring the sensations of each step:

- Notice the changing sensations as you lift and place the feet on the ground. Notice whether you have a tendency to walk on the side of the sole. Notice which part of your foot first touches the ground and which part is last to lift. Notice the subtle movements of your toes. Notice the changing balance of the body from side to side.
- There may also be awareness of the space in which you move. Be curious about how it feels to walk with different footwear or barefoot and how different surfaces feel. Allow an awareness of the changing views and sounds, moment to moment experiences, constantly flowing and changing.
- It is likely that you will notice that your mind wanders

into thinking or becomes distracted by sounds, sights or smells. Just notice when this happens and gently bring your attention back to the physical sensations of each step.

- Mindful walking can be practiced as a formal meditation, indoors or outdoors, choosing a space to walk back and forth or in a circle. It can also be practiced informally, when we are going about our daily lives, letting go of thoughts about our destination or where we have been and just bringing our attention to each step on our journey.

- As with the previous movement exercises, mindful movement can, if you wish, follow the natural ebb and flow of the breath.

Mark's Story: The Joy of Movement

I have always enjoyed a range of movement-based activities. I used to play football, badminton, and squash on a regular basis. Unfortunately, I was not particularly proficient and would negatively judge my ability compared to the opposition or my teammates. Not only would I judge myself, but this would sometimes be reinforced by members of my own team! At university I took up ballroom dancing and ju-jitsu, but these too led to doubts regarding my ability. With dancing I was told I had a unique style and, although I have occasionally been praised, being told that my dancing looked like 'Mr Bean on acid' did not boost my confidence! With martial arts, first ju-jitsu, then kung fu and latterly Tai Chi, I occasionally found the rigidity of set sequences stifling and restrictive. Again, judgements about whether I was doing it right hindered my progress.

I then discovered the joy of mindful movement. More a moving meditation than exercise, mindful movement is just moving for the sake of moving. There is no right or wrong, as the focus is just to notice what any movement feels like. Any movement can be mindful. One of my favourite mindful movement practices is simply walking and focusing on the physical sensations of each step, with no destination in mind, just walking for the sake of walking. There is no judgement, just awareness of sensations, moment by moment, one movement at a time.

Mindful movement is my go-to meditation when I feel stressed or under pressure. When I feel the need to calm my mind I will get up and just walk or repeat some simple arm movements in time with my breath. Whenever I have had periods of struggle maintaining a regular formal meditation practice, it has always been mindful movement that has reinforced my practice. In 2015 I was diagnosed with Crohn's disease. When I was first diagnosed the pain and discomfort of the condition often meant that I struggled with body awareness and breathing meditations but with mindful movement I could always find a place of stillness.

More recently the practice of moving non-judgmentally inspired me and gave me the confidence at the age of 55 to train as a yoga teacher. For me, yoga is a form of mindful movement because I am bringing awareness to the felt sensations of my body as I practice. It is not about being perfect or being the most flexible in the room, but it is about finding a place of stillness and meditation in movement.

Body Awareness: The Body Scan

In the body scan meditation, we systematically bring our attention to felt sensations in each part of the body in turn. This practice enables us to notice tension and let go, which can often help us to relax. But if you don't feel relaxed don't worry. The aim is to simply be aware of what is.

The body scan meditation is an opportunity to practice non-judgement. We may notice pleasant sensations or unpleasant sensations. There may be areas of the body with no sensations at all. None of this is right or wrong it just is. See if you can observe with curiosity.

Preparation

- Find a comfortable lying or sitting position. Most people find that the practice is best done lying down.
- If you are lying, make sure that you are lying on something comfortable such as your bed or a yoga mat. It is good to have a cushion to support your head that is at the right height for your neck.
- Make sure that you are warm enough - perhaps have a blanket nearby.
- Usually this is done lying on the back with the legs outstretched. If you have a lower back difficulty, then it can help to bend the knees and have the feet flat on the ground or bed. However, the most important thing is to listen to your own body and find a position that works for you. And if you need to move just do so!

The Meditation

- Begin with a broad sense of the whole body, particularly noticing contact with the ground. Allow your weight to sink into your support so that you can have a sense of being grounded.
- Notice the felt sensations of the breath, without controlling or forcing, but allowing the breath to be an anchor for the remainder of the practice.
- Then, take your awareness to each part of the body in turn and notice the sensations that you feel. You may begin at the toes and work your way up or you may prefer to start at the head and work your way down. As with all mindfulness practices, there is no right or wrong way to practice!
- If you become aware of tension in the body, see if you can let it go, or imagine the muscle relaxing and softening.
- If you become aware of pain or discomfort, see if you can soften any of the tension you may be holding around it, and be curious about the sensation with kindness and interest, rather than blocking against the feeling. You might wish to explore using the breath to soothe.
- If you don't feel any sensation at all that is fine too. What is important is simply to be aware. There is no right or wrong way to feel!
- If you become distracted, this means that you are human! When you notice a distraction, this is a moment of

awareness. Take this opportunity to gently bring your awareness back to the body.

- If sensations are pleasant see if you can appreciate them. We often take pleasant aspects of our lives for granted so take this opportunity to savour the simple but pleasant experiences.

Lesson Two: Summary

Developing a regular practice means building a new habit. It takes time so celebrate your achievement when you remember to practice rather than being self-critical when you don't.

We automatically judge our experience as pleasant, unpleasant, or neutral. And it is normal to judge. However, liking or disliking something does not make it right or wrong; good or bad. It just is what it is. Practicing non-judgement means noticing your automatic judgements and not reacting to them.

Awareness of the body can help us to release tension, increase awareness of emotions, and become more present. Increased awareness also enables us to listen to wat our bodies need and respond accordingly. By bringing an appreciative awareness to the body we can connect with all that our bodies can do and experience rather than focusing solely on negative judgements.

Mindful movement involves focusing our awareness to notice physical and mental sensations as we move, which reinforces the mind body connection. Our bodies reflect our internal experience as much as our minds respond to our physical experiences.

Home Practice

This week see if you can bring your attention to the physical sensations of some everyday activities. We suggest that you shift the spotlight of your attention to the physical sensations for a few moments 3-4 times a day as you go about your usual activities. As you do the activity and notice the physical sensations also notice whether the sensations feel pleasant, unpleasant or neutral. Make a note in your journal of your observations.

Alternate your practice between formal mindful movement and the body scan each day. We suggest you try these meditations at different times during the day. You might notice that your experience is different in the morning compared with the afternoon or evening. Make a note of anything you notice in your journal.

Questions for Reflection

Q1. What happens when you let go of judgement in your meditation?

Q2. What happens when you let go of judgement in your everyday life?

Q3. What gets in the way of your practice of non-judgement?

7

lesson three: gratitude

In lesson three we begin by exploring some of the challenges that we might experience when practising the body scan meditation. Although the body scan can be relaxing, this is not always the case. If you experience discomfort, distraction or find yourself falling asleep this does not mean you are doing it wrong!

This lesson's attitude is gratitude. We have a tendency to notice the negative and ignore the positive aspects of our experience. However, by practicing gratitude we can begin to notice the pleasant and positive around us and, ultimately this can make us happier!

In this lesson we also consider how to practice gratitude in our everyday lives. We introduce two practices. The first is the gratitude meditation, which is an opportunity to reflect on experiences that we appreciate. The second practice is the gratitude body scan, which is an opportunity to observe the body and appreciate all that it can do for us.

Home Practice Review: Some Common Challenges in the Body Scan

In lesson two we introduced the body scan meditation. Hopefully you have had the opportunity to practice this a few times during the last week. And you may have noticed a range of experiences.

1. You may have noticed physical pain or discomfort. Often when we experience pain, we do whatever we can to distract ourselves from it. If we experience pain or discomfort in a body awareness meditation this can be challenging. You might find it helpful to change your posture or gently move the body to release tension. You might imagine that as you breathe in, the breath is reaching and soothing the pain and as you breathe out releasing tension you may be holding in the area around the pain. You might see if you can be curious about the pain, perhaps noticing if it changes in any way. See if you can bring a non-judgemental awareness to a feeling that you don't like. And if the pain or discomfort is too intense then maybe the body scan isn't right for you at this time. It is ok to stop and come back to it when you are ready.

2. You may have noticed your mind starting to wander. This is normal. When we meditate, we are getting to know our minds, and this includes becoming aware of our tendency to become distracted. When you notice that

you have become caught up in thoughts, see if you can acknowledge the thought and let it go and come back to the meditation. You might need to do this a hundred times in one meditation and that is absolutely fine!

3. You might find that you fall asleep during a body scan. This is also normal. This might be your body's way of saying that you are tired. However, the aim of the meditation is not to fall asleep so you might try opening your eyes for a few moments during the body scan if you feel that you might nod off. If this happens regularly, then you could try the practice in a sitting position, with your back upright and, if sitting on a chair sitting slightly forward so the back supports itself. Alternatively, you might change the time of day that you practice the meditation. For example, you might avoid doing a body scan after a heavy meal.

4. Perhaps you tried the body scan once or twice and decided that you didn't like it and so it isn't for you. We would really encourage you to persevere. If you hate it and find it a real struggle, then we wouldn't ask you to force yourself. However, if you are put off because you don't love it straight away, please stick at it. The more we practice the more we learn about our bodies, our judgements and our default reactions and the more we will benefit.

Gratitude

When eating fruit, remember the one who planted the tree.
Vietnamese Proverb

Imagine you have been out on a shopping trip. You went to five different shops. In four shops you found the exact thing you were looking for; it was in the sale and the shop assistants were helpful. In one shop you couldn't find what you were looking for and the shop assistant was rude when you asked for help. How do you look back on the day's events? Do you remember the four positive experiences or the one negative one?

If you think back over the last 24 hours, do you remember the things that went wrong or the things that went well? We tend to notice the negative more than the positive. This is known as negativity bias, and it has an evolutionary purpose. Negativity bias, our inbuilt tendency to notice the negative, helps us to avoid danger. This was particularly useful early in human evolution. However, this tendency means that we don't always notice the positive, and we miss out on the richness of life.

However, we can change this! The practice of gratitude is the antidote to negativity bias. By focusing on something positive or pleasant for at least 12 seconds, it can actually have a physical impact on the brain!

Gratitude is a practice that we can choose to develop. It does not mean ignoring the bad stuff. Rather it means putting the difficulties into context so that we are better equipped to cope. At the end of a day, can we think of the things that have gone well rather than only focusing on what went wrong, or what we could have done better?

The hedonic treadmill is the idea that whenever we gain something new – such as a new car, a new pair of shoes or a pay rise, although we might be happy at first, we quickly return to a base level of happiness. This means that we need more 'stuff' in order to feel the same short-lived happiness. And if we seek pleasure in this way we will never be satisfied. However, when we practice gratitude, we appreciate what we already have, giving a sense of richness and abundance. We recognise all the things that we take for granted and take pleasure in the small things.

Gratitude can have a positive impact on our relationships. We learn to appreciate others rather than focusing on (and even pointing out) their faults. This can make us a lot nicer to be around! Of course, practising gratitude doesn't mean ignoring the difficulties in a relationship, particularly if your friend, colleague, or partner is behaving in a way that is inappropriate or abusive. We can practice gratitude and maintain boundaries.

Gratitude doesn't mean that everything is rosy. There will always be challenges and difficulties. But gratitude and appreciation can help us to gain perspective, cope with life's difficulties and lead happier lives. There is something pleasant in every moment, however small, if we choose to look for it. Sometimes this is easier than others!

The Gratitude Meditation

There are lots of ways to practice a gratitude meditation. This version focuses specifically on cultivating a sense of gratitude and appreciation for the everyday things that we take for granted connected with our home and the infrastructure of where we live. Remember that we are not forcing ourselves to feel a particular way. Instead, we are setting an intention towards gratitude and connecting with the possibility that there are things to appreciate:

- Find a comfortable relaxed meditation seated position with the back upright and supporting itself, but not too rigid. You might sit with your feet flat on the floor, hands gently resting in your lap.
- At the start of this meditation allow your eyes to remain open with a soft focus.
- Set an intention to be present and cultivate a sense of gratitude for the place you are in and all the things that support you in this world.
- Start by turning your attention to the breath, noticing what it feels like to breathe. Notice what feels like to breathe in and notice what it feels like to breathe out.
- Without straining or forcing, allow the breath to lengthen and deepen, taking five or six longer deeper breaths. See if you can allow a sense of appreciation for the breath.
- Now notice the contact with the surfaces supporting you, maybe allowing a sense of being held and supported unconditionally by the ground beneath you. Give thanks for the support of the chair or floor supporting you.

- Open up to the space around you, slowly looking round the room you are in. You might notice décor, art, books, or furniture. Notice the things in the room that bring you comfort, pleasure and joy. Bring a sense of appreciation and gratitude for this space you are in right now and the support and comfort it brings.

- Notice the simple things in this room that you may take for granted: the walls, ceiling, doors offering shelter, safety, and security; the heating bringing warmth; the electricity bringing light; the broadband enabling communication.

- Say a silent thank you and maybe allow the eyes to close as you bring to mind the other rooms in the building you are in right now.

- Open up your awareness to the people and/or animals you share this building with. You might reflect on family, housemates, and pets, appreciating the love and companionship they offer you. Appreciating the people you welcome into your space, friends and loved ones, appreciating the support and comfort they bring you.

- Bring to mind the space around this building and the infrastructures that enable this space to work for you: the road networks providing access; the sewage, water, gas, electricity networks that provide essential utilities; the facilities available to you to purchase food, clothes, equipment. Reflect on the services that support and protect you, such as: refuse collection, postal service, police, and the health service. You might reflect on all the people involved in making this all possible. You might appreciate the farmers, the transport workers, to all the people you don't know that support you. Bringing appreciation to this connection to all the people involved in giving you this space where you can feel safe and comforted. Give thanks for all they do for you.

- Allow a sense of appreciation and gratitude for this connection. Even when we are sitting alone, we are connected to so many things and so many people.
- Now say a silent thank you to this space and its connection to everything as you bring the practice to a close.

How to Practice Gratitude

There are lots of ways we can practice gratitude. The list of suggestions below is far from exhaustive. Be creative and see what you can come up with!

1. **Keep a gratitude journal.** Each evening, write down the things that you are grateful for that day. These might be very simple things such as a kind word from a friend or loved one; noticing a beautiful sunset; or enjoying a cup of tea. At first it might be difficult to think of things to be grateful for because of our tendency to focus on the negative. However, in time we learn to notice more and more things to appreciate. And the act of writing helps to imprint the positive in your mind.

   Of course, we won't always feel positive and grateful. On days when you are feeling down, read through your gratitude journal and notice how this feels. Remember you are not trying to force a feeling. However, even if it feels like going through the motions at times, you are planting seeds of gratitude that will bear fruit in the future.

2. **Try a gratitude body scan.** When you practice the body scan, which we introduced in lesson two, see if you can appreciate all that your body can do for you. For example, when you notice your eyes, appreciate the ability to see. When you notice your legs and feet, appreciate every step that you take. We tend to notice all our aches and pains but overlook what is right with our bodies. As Jon Kabat-Zinn has said, 'if you are here and you are breathing, there is more right with you than there is wrong.' Notice how it feels to appreciate your body.

3. **Take yourself for a gratitude walk.** Next time you go for a walk - perhaps taking a walk to work or taking the dog for a walk, see if you can find something beautiful in your surroundings to appreciate. Instead of distracting yourself by listening to music or podcasts, take in the sights and sounds around you and allow your walk to be a full sensory experience. See if you can notice the architecture around you or observe the signs of the changing seasons by looking at the trees around you. Listen to ambient sounds and see if you can notice birdsong or other pleasant sounds. You do not need to be walking in the countryside to find things to appreciate. Wherever you are, there is always something to be grateful for.

Rachel's Story: Choosing Gratitude

In March 2020 I moved house after the breakdown of a relationship. The relationship had been an unhappy one for both of us for some time, but it was still a painful experience for it to end. It was also quite a daunting experience for me because it meant living on my own for the first time, after living with a partner or housemates for my entire adult life. Although I wasn't entirely alone because I moved with my cat, Sheema! Within a fortnight of moving the UK went into lockdown due to the Covid19 pandemic. I was living on my own, grieving the loss of a relationship and I couldn't even go out and see my friends! I worked from home, providing mindfulness classes online and I only went out to go to the supermarket. Then in January 2021, in spite of being careful, I caught Covid.

The pandemic was a shared collective experience that impacted us all, but in different ways. It has been devastating for many people, particularly those who lost loved ones or are living with the effects of long covid. However, I feel that I had a choice throughout this entire strange time. I could choose to focus on the losses, or I could choose gratitude.

Although the end of the relationship was painful, I knew it was for the best for both of us. And lockdown provided the opportunity to heal. I couldn't go out and distract myself. Instead, I spent time in quiet stillness, decorating my home, and getting to know myself again. Lockdown provided the opportunity to spend quality time with Sheema. As a house cat I think she really appreciated the extra attention! Working from home meant that I was forced to learn new skills that I didn't know that I wanted to learn. I gained confidence to make videos for YouTube, to record 'Facebook Lives' and to deliver classes on Zoom.

Even when I caught Covid I had a choice about how to look at it. I could feel really unlucky for catching it in spite of being careful. Or I could be grateful that my symptoms were mild. I was exhausted for *a few days and needed to take extra naps but otherwise I have been fortunate. And I am also grateful for the infrastructure that allowed me to access online shopping while I was self-isolating*

I am grateful for technology that has meant I can do Zumba classes online with my mum and catch up with my friends in the evenings. I am grateful for the views from my living room windows that seem to change every day. I am also grateful that I am able to choose gratitude.

Gratitude Body Scan

In the gratitude body scan, we observe the felt sensations of the body as with a regular body scan. However, we also connect with a sense of gratitude and appreciation for the body. This might include reflecting on what the body can do.

- Find a comfortable relaxed meditation position. This can be either sitting or lying down. Close your eyes if that feels comfortable for you and tune into the weight of the body. Scan the body for any tension and let go of this if you can.
- Gently turn your attention to the breath. Notice what it feels like to breathe in and notice what it feels like to breathe out.
- Notice a broad sense of the breath. Notice all the parts of the body that are moved by the breath.
- Throughout this practice allow the breath to act as an anchor to enable you to maintain focus.
- If at any time you notice that your mind has wandered, acknowledge where the mind went, and gently bring your attention back to the breath and back to the body.
- Now take your attention down through the body to the

feet and legs. Bring your attention to any physical sensations you notice in the feet and legs.

- You might notice how sensations continually change, how they come and go. There may be some strong sensations, some subtle sensations, and some parts of the legs and feet where there are no sensations. That's ok! We are not trying to make anything happen. Just notice what sensations are there for you in this moment.

- Whilst maintaining awareness of the physical sensations in the feet and legs, bring to mind all of the things your feet and legs do for you, allow a sense of appreciation for the feet and legs. Thank your feet and legs for the ability to stand, walk run and anything else that comes to mind.

- Now letting go of your legs and feet, shift your attention to the torso and, whist noticing physical sensations, bring a sense of appreciation to the torso. You might thank the torso for the organs and systems in this part of the body. You might thank the digestive system, the heart, the lungs, or you might offer thanks to the spine and ribs for supporting you and protecting the vital organs.

- Now letting go of the torso gently shift the spotlight of your attention to the arms and hands. As before, focusing attention on the physical sensations and bringing appreciation to all that the arms and hands do for you. You may also include the sense of touch. Offer thanks to the arms and hands for all you appreciate about them.

- Finally bring your attention to your head, repeating the process of appreciation and including the senses of taste, smell, sight and hearing, the gift of speech and the brain. See if you can appreciate the ability to think, understand

and communicate. You might even appreciate the ability to appreciate!

- Now slowly expand the spotlight of your awareness to the whole body and give thanks to all that it does for you.
- In your own time let go of the practice, perhaps noticing whether you feel different compared to when you first started. Notice any sounds around you and open your eyes whenever you are ready.

Lesson Three - Summary

Negativity bias is the human tendency to notice the negative and overlook the positive. The practice of gratitude is an antidote to negativity bias. The practice of gratitude does not mean that we ignore the unpleasant aspects of our lives, but it helps us to put our difficulties into perspective and helps us to cope.

Gratitude can be practised in many ways, including a gratitude meditation or a gratitude body scan. We can also make a note of things that we are grateful for in a gratitude journal or notice the pleasant aspects of our surroundings during a gratitude walk.

Home Practice

This week see if you practice either a gratitude meditation or a gratitude body scan each day. If you have time, you might even choose to do both practices! As with all mindfulness activities, this is a form of brain training, so the more regularly we practice, the more effective the training. Make a note in your journal of your observations. You might also begin a daily gratitude journal, observing and making a note of pleasant experiences that you have noticed that day.

Questions for Reflection

Q1. How do you feel when you practice gratitude?

Q2. What are the barriers to practising and expressing gratitude?

lesson four: acceptance

This lesson's attitude is acceptance. This attitude is particularly important when developing a meditation practice. When we practice a gratitude meditation for example, as introduced in the previous lesson, we might always not feel the pleasant emotions that we would like. This is where acceptance comes in. What we feel is what we feel.

This lesson's practices involve learning to gently turn our attention towards difficult experiences and meeting them with kindness and compassion, rather than fighting against reality.

This lesson also focuses on understanding the mechanisms of breathing and the value of breath awareness. This lesson includes several 'breath enquiries' – experiments to enable us to understand our breath more fully. This culminates in a breathing body scan, a meditation practice in which we explore sensations of breathing in different parts of the body.

Home Practice Review: The Intention of Gratitude

In lesson three we introduced the attitude of gratitude and introduced two practices to help you to connect with gratitude and appreciation in your everyday life. Sometimes gratitude feels easier than others. On some days you might find it quite straightforward to come up with examples of experiences that you appreciate.

On some days this might feel more challenging. Perhaps you are aware of things that you could be grateful for, but you simply don't feel it today. That is absolutely fine! It is important to remember that we are not trying to force ourselves to feel a particular way. How you feel is how you feel. By connecting with the possibility of gratitude we are connecting with a powerful intention to notice the positive and connecting with an intention to be grateful. In time and with regular practice this will become easier, and you will begin to notice more and more things to appreciate.

Acceptance

Grant me the serenity to accept the things I cannot change;
the courage to change the things I can;
and the wisdom to know the difference.
The Serenity Prayer

According to stoic philosophy, the only control we really have is over what we think and what we do. Our actions may have an impact on the world around us, but we cannot guarantee the outcome. Ultimately, we can choose to react and fight against our experience, or we can choose to accept the reality of the present moment and respond creatively.

Acceptance does not mean that you are satisfied with things as they are or that you are resigned to tolerating things as they "have to be." It does not mean that you should abandon your principles and values or abandon your desire to change and grow. Acceptance can form the springboard for change because you are much more likely to know what to do and to have the inner conviction to act when you have a clear picture of what is actually happening.

This applies to both our internal and external experience. Self-acceptance does not mean we resign ourselves to being a particular "type' of person, 'it's just the way I am'. For example, you might notice that you are angry and tell yourself that you are an angry person and that is just the way you are. You might use that to justify flying off the handle and becoming aggressive.

However, this is a misunderstanding of acceptance. We can't choose how we feel (although we can plant seeds that might impact on how we will feel in future, as we will go on to explore), but we can choose how to respond. In other words, we can accept feeling angry, but we do not need to accept that we will fly off the handle.

Acceptance is the balanced response to what is happening, the space between reacting and blocking. And it is in that space where we can choose our response. Self-acceptance is the foundation for understanding and getting to know ourselves.

It does not mean accepting external experience that is leading to suffering. For example, you may enjoy the work that you do but the culture of the organisation means you don't like going to work. Acceptance doesn't mean putting up with a negative work culture, it is not acquiescence, nor does it mean giving up a job you enjoy. It could be either or there may be other alternatives. Meaningful change is only possible when we allow ourselves to see the whole picture, to clearly see the facts as they are in this moment opens up the possibility of growth and change.

We may find some of our relationships challenging. Unfortunately, we cannot change other people, but we can make a choice about how we respond. By accepting the aspect of others that we cannot change, we can choose to respond to them more creatively.

In meditation we practice acceptance by bringing our attention to what is happening as it is happening without expecting or wishing things to be different. we may often find meditation relaxing and calming, but sometimes it might not be and that's ok, just accept this meditation experience as it is with a sense of kindly curiosity.

In any moment ask yourself what is actually happening and what do you have a choice about. What can you change and what can you accept?

Moving Towards a Difficult Experience

We often ignore or push away things that we find difficult. Alternatively, we often obsess over difficulties and dwell on things that we cannot change. In the following practice, we consciously turn our attention towards something that we find difficult and notice how it feels in the present moment.

We might turn our attention to a pain or discomfort that is already present. See if you can observe the sensations of pain in the present moment without getting caught up in a story about the pain.

Alternatively, you might choose to recall something stressful that has happened recently and notice the sensations and emotions that are evoked. You might recall an argument or a criticism for example. When we remember and think about something challenging it often evokes strong physical and emotional responses in the present moment. For this practice, the invitation is to pay attention to these responses with a sense of interest and curiosity rather than getting caught up in a story about the situation.

The aim is not to fix the situation or make ourselves feel better. Nor are we passively condoning a situation that might need resolving at some other time. Instead, the aim is to observe the difficulty in the moment and accept that this is your experience.

At any point if the practice feels too much, you can go back to focusing on your breath.

- Establish a comfortable, dignified meditation posture. Lightly close your eyes if that feels comfortable for you.
- Focus your attention on your breath. Allow your breath to be an anchor that you can return to at any point if the practice feels too challenging.
- When you are ready, bring to mind something that you

are finding difficult. You might choose to connect with a challenging memory. Instead of getting caught up in the story of the memory, see if you can stay with your present moment experience as you bring it to mind. Alternatively, you might choose to focus on a physical pain or discomfort.

- Explore the difficulty. How does it feel in the body? Does it have a colour, a texture, a shape? See if you can focus on how it feels in the present moment rather than using your thinking to try to solve the problem. Bring a sense of curiosity to your experience.

- When you are ready, let the difficulty go and return your attention to the breath. Open your eyes when you are ready and bring the practice to a close.

Compassionate Acceptance

In the above meditation, we learn to move towards a difficult experience. The following meditation builds upon this and is based on the self-compassion break by Kristin Neff. According to Kristin Neff, compassion is a kindly response to suffering and has three elements. In order to have compassion, we need:

1. **Awareness** of the suffering we are experiencing;
2. A recognition that suffering is part of **being human;**
3. A sense of **kindness.**

- Establish a comfortable, dignified meditation posture. Lightly close your eyes if that feels comfortable for you.

- Focus your attention on your breath. Allow your breath to be an anchor that you can return to at any point if the practice feels too challenging.

- When you are ready, bring to mind something in your life that you are finding difficult or stressful. Notice your emotional response. Notice how it feels in the body. For example, you might notice an anxious feeling in your chest, or butterflies in your stomach.

- As you notice your experience instead of resisting it, try acknowledging it by saying to yourself: 'This is unpleasant. This is painful This is a moment of suffering,' or whatever words feel right for you.

- When you are ready, see if you can connect with a sense of shared humanity. You might say to yourself: 'This is part of being human. Everyone feels like this sometimes. It is ok to feel like this,' or whatever words feel right or you

- See if you can meet your suffering with kindness. You might place your hands over your heart, or the part of the body that feels unpleasant. Feel the gentle warmth of the touch. You might say to yourself 'May I be kind to myself. "May I be compassionate towards myself,' or anything else that works for you.

- When you are ready, let the difficulty go and return your attention to the breath. Open your eyes when you are ready and bring the practice to a close.

Mark's Story: Managing my Chronic illness

As previously mentioned, I live with a chronic illness, an inflammatory bowel condition called Crohn's disease. The symptoms include regular periods of abdominal pain and discomfort among others. Unfortunately, due to a severe allergic reaction to the recommended medication, I do not currently receive any medical treatment for my condition. For over five years I have managed the pain and discomfort with mindfulness practice. In particular, the attitude of bringing a kindly acceptance to my experience and symptoms has transformed my relationship with my illness.

At any given moment I am aware of sensations in the side of my abdomen. These range from mild discomfort to quite severe pain. It would be easy for me to focus on these sensations and wallow in my discomfort. Or to try and distract myself and block out the pain. However, by accepting the reality of the situation with kindness, I am able to respond to changes in my symptoms without it defining me.

I use the compassionate acceptance practice regularly to respond to my condition. Before I received a diagnosis, I started using compassionate acceptance to self soothe. Whilst lying in hospital not knowing what was causing the pain and realising that I had no control over what was happening, I remembered having felt this way before. When my daughter, Lydia, was about four years old she was admitted to hospital with a rare autoimmune disease that caused severe pain in all of her joints. I remember sitting with her through the night desperately wanting to make her pain go away. All I could do was be there for her, give her a hug, tell her that she was loved and that the pain will pass. My being there did not lessen the pain but it did make it more bearable for her. Thankfully she made a complete recovery. For the past five *years, whenever I have a flare up, I respond to my intestines in the same way. I gently place my hand on my abdomen, I acknowledge the pain, I offer compassionate love and accept that the pain will pass.*

Bringing compassionate acceptance to my pain does not reduce the pain but it does reduce my suffering and make it more bearable.

Understanding the Breath - Why Breath Awareness is Important

From the moment we are born we breathe. Depending on our age, what we are doing, and how we are feeling we take anything between 17000 and 50000 breaths per day. That is a lot of breaths! Fortunately, most of the time we breathe on autopilot, so we don't need to think about the breath or consciously do anything to breathe. Consequently, most of us, most of the time take it for granted and don't pay it very much attention. However, the ebb and flow of the breath is literally the rhythm of our life. We can survive weeks without food, days without water but only minutes without the breath.

Although we breathe automatically, the rhythm of our breath and how we breathe changes depending on our emotional state, our mental state, and our physical state. For example, when we feel stressed, we take faster, shallower breaths and when we are relaxed, we breathe deeper slower breaths.

Unlike most other automatic bodily functions, we can easily switch from autopilot to actively changing the breath. We can hold our breath, we can shorten or deepen our breath and we can regulate our breath. How we breathe can affect heart rate, blood pressure, stress levels, digestion and general health and wellbeing. There are numerous breathing techniques have been developed to manage pain, aid relaxation, and improve well-being.

One of the eight limbs of the practice of Yoga, Pranyama, is devoted to different breathing techniques.

In most mindfulness meditation practices we are not changing the breath in any way - we are just paying attention to it. However, by bringing our awareness to the breath we can begin to understand it and understand how we are feeling in that moment. Outside of formal practice, if we are more aware of how we are breathing, this creates the opportunity to change how we are breathing, and potentially how we are feeling. Often at the start of a meditation we take some longer deeper breaths. Deep slow gentle breaths signal to the body that we are safe, the body can relax, and the mind can settle. However, for the most part, mindfulness meditation involves maintaining a focus on the breath without manipulating it or changing it in any way. Mindfulness of the breath can be practiced at any time. The breath is always with us - we can't go anywhere without it!

For some people who have experienced difficulties breathing, the very thought of paying attention to the breath can bring on feelings of anxiety, judgements about whether they are breathing properly and a tendency to try to change the breath. However, with persistent practice the breath can again become a friend.

Breath Enquiries:

1. **Breathing In For Four and Out For Six**

Usually when we invite you to observe the breath in mindfulness meditation, we suggest that you keep the breath natural and observe it just as it is. However, for this next exercise the invitation is to control the length of your breath, breathing in for the count of four and breathing out for the count of six. The reason for this is that focusing on the out-breath stimulates the parasympathetic nervous system, the part of our nervous system associated with relaxation and down-regulation. By lengthening the out-breath you may find that you become more relaxed - but don't worry if you don't! There's no right or wrong way to feel!

- Find yourself a comfortable seated position. You might choose to sit with your feet flat on the floor and your back upright with your eyes lightly closed. But choose a posture that feels right for you.
- Connect with a sense of being grounded - notice the contact you can feel with the floor, your chair or whatever is supporting you.
- When you are ready turn your attention to the breath. Initially, just allow your breath to be as it is.
- When you are ready, bring in the counting. Allow your in-breath to be natural and count to four as you inhale. As you breathe out, see if you can lengthen the out-breath and breathe out for the count of six.
- Continue focusing on the breath. If you become distracted, just notice the thought, let it go and come back to the breath.
- Notice how you feel as you focus on the breath in this way.
- When you are ready, let go of the counting and return to your regular breathing pattern.

- Notice the sounds around you, open your eyes when you're ready and bring the meditation to a close.

1. **Abdominal Breathing**

The diaphragm, in the middle of the chest works tirelessly to enable us to breathe. When we breathe in, the diaphragm flattens, pushing the organs of the abdomen outwards. This creates a vacuum in the lungs so that air can rush in. When we breathe out, the diaphragm domes, the abdominal organs return to their original position and the air rushes out. So, our bellies go out on the in-breath and go in on the out-breath. However, often we inhibit our breathing and breathe too shallowly, hold our breath, or overly rely on auxiliary muscles in the chest.

In this next exercise you are invited to focus on the breath in the abdomen. Don't worry if you don't feel movement in the abdomen straight away. This might take practice and however you are breathing is good enough!

- Find yourself a comfortable seated position. You might choose to sit with your feet flat on the floor and your back upright with your eyes lightly closed. But choose a posture that feels right for you.
- Connect with a sense of being grounded - notice the contact you can feel with the floor, your chair or whatever is supporting you.
- When you are ready place your hands on your abdomen so that the fingertips are lightly touching. See if you can feel your fingertips separate as you breathe in and go back

together as you breathe out. If you can't feel this, you might try imagining breathing into your abdomen.

- Notice how it feels to focus on the breath in your abdomen.
- When you are ready, bring your hands to rest in your lap.
- Notice the sounds around you, and in your own time open your eyes and bring the meditation to a close.

1. Breathing Body Scan

In the breathing body scan we focus specifically on breathing sensations in different parts of the body. We don't change how we breathe in order to feel these sensations. We simply notice what is there. Some sensations will be more subtle than others. And in certain areas you might not notice anything at all. That is absolutely fine. You also might notice that focusing on some areas has an effect on your focus and concentration, while focusing on other areas feels more relaxing. As always, there is no right or wrong way to feel.

- Find a comfortable relaxed meditation position. This can be either sitting or lying down. Close your eyes and tune into the weight of the body. Scan the body for any tension and let go of this if you can.
- Gently turn your attention to the breath. Notice what it feels like to breathe in and notice what it feels like to breathe out. Notice a broad sense of the breath. Notice all the parts of the body that are moved by each breath.

Notice which areas there are strong sensations and where sensations are more subtle.

- As you begin to focus the spotlight of your attention on particular parts of the breath, be curious about the different effects of focusing on the breath in different parts of the body. Notice which areas feel most soothing and relaxing and which areas feel most energising.

- Firstly, take your attention to any sensations of the breath in the nostrils. Notice how it feels to focus in this area. How is your energy? Mood? Concentration?

- Take your attention to any sensations of the breath in the mouth. Notice how it feels to focus in this area. How is your energy? Mood? Concentration?

- Take your attention to any sensations of the breath in the throat area. Notice how it feels to focus in this area. How is your energy? Mood? Concentration?

- Take your attention to any sensations of the breath in the chest and ribcage. You might notice the breath in the front or the sides of the ribs. Notice how it feels to focus in this area. How is your energy? Mood? Concentration?

- Take your attention to any sensations of the breath in the back of the ribcage. Notice how it feels to focus in this area. How is your energy? Mood? Concentration?

- Take your attention to any echoes of the breath in the lower back. You might notice a gentle rocking sensation here. Notice how it feels to focus in this area. How is your energy? Mood? Concentration?

- Take your attention to any sensations of the breath in the abdomen. This might be quite a large sensation, or it might be more subtle. Notice how it feels to focus in this area. How is your energy? Mood? Concentration?

- Now broaden your awareness to take in the whole of the breath again. Perhaps you now have a favourite place to focus on. You might choose to rest your awareness here.

- When you are ready bring the practice to a close and open your eyes.

Summary

How you feel is how you feel! We cannot force ourselves to feel differently. Often by accepting how we are feeling right now, this is more likely to change.

The only control we really have is over what we think and what we do. Ultimately, we can choose to react and fight against our experience, or we can choose to accept the reality of the present moment and respond creatively. We can still make a difference, but we cannot force other people or our external circumstances to change.

We instinctively want to turn away from our difficulties or we want to fight against them. However, when we learn to be with our difficulties with compassion, we discover just how resilient we are. We stop beating ourselves up and let go of tension.

The breath is a wonderful tool for developing self-awareness. We can use the breath to help us to recognise stress and tension and to help us to let go. In the breathing body scan we explore sensations of the breath in different parts of the body. By getting to know the breath you can learn to breathe more optimally and learn to use your breath to self soothe.

Home practice

This week see if you practice a breathing body scan each day. Sometimes you might try the practice sitting and other times you might try lying down. Notice how the change in posture impacts on your experience of the breath and of the meditation. And in your everyday life, whenever you find yourself becoming caught up in something unpleasant or challenging, see if you can practice a compassionate acceptance meditation. You might not remember to do the practice in the moment, particularly if the difficulty is very challenging. In this case, you might choose to recall the difficulty afterwards and see what happens when you bring compassion to the memory. As always, make a note of your observations in your journal.

Questions for Reflection

Q1. Do you find that some things are easier to accept than others? Why do you think this is?

Q2. What happens when you fight reality?

lesson five:
non-striving

This lesson's attitude is non-striving. This does not mean that we give up. Instead, non-striving means approaching our meditation and our lives with a balanced effort. This is particularly important when managing thoughts in meditation. When we meditate, we are not trying to empty our minds or force thoughts out. However, our intention is not to become carried away by our thoughts. Instead, we find a balance in which we acknowledge thoughts and let them go. In this lesson we introduce a breathing meditation in which we use counting as an anchor to help us to stay focused on the sensations of breathing.

In this lesson we also explore non-striving in movement using the concept of the 'soft edge' and the 'hard edge' of movement. Rather than pushing ourselves too hard - or remaining too firmly within our comfort zone - taking a mindful approach enables us to practice balanced effort.

Home practice review

In lesson four we introduced the attitude of acceptance. We introduced breathing practices and the practice of turning towards difficult experiences and meeting them with compassion and acceptance.

Common practice issues:

1. *Am I breathing right?*

   The support of the breath is beneficial to mindfulness practice because it is easily accessible. The breath is always available. However, the intention is to maintain a *light* awareness of the breath. When we focus too tightly on the breath, it is common to start judging the breath and trying to change it. It is important to accept the breath as it is in the moment rather than bringing expectations of how the breath should feel or where you should feel it. If you are breathing, you are doing it right!

2. *Becoming overwhelmed by unpleasant experiences*

   Turning towards difficult experiences whether physical, emotional, or psychological is challenging and is an act of bravery. However, this is not a reckless act of 'diving in.' Rather, it is a gentle, cautious approach with awareness. The more acute the distress, whether physical or emotional, the greater the risk of overwhelm. When it starts to feel too uncomfortable, pull back and return to the support of the breath.

3. *There is nothing to fix!*

We are not trying to 'fix' or stop our suffering. Often, we add to our suffering because of our attempts to fix it. However, by acknowledging it with compassionate acceptance we can manage it and respond more effectively.

4. *Don't beat yourself up for beating yourself up!*

We all make mistakes, and our natural negativity bias can lead to self-criticism and negative self-judgement. Knowing this does not stop it happening, but we don't have to compound it with further self-criticism for not being mindful! By bringing awareness to our default reactions, we can start choosing healthier responses. However, this takes practice!

5. *Don't look for suffering!*

Suffering is inevitable but not a constant. Practices where we turn towards a difficulty or compassionate acceptance exercises are there for when there is already suffering. If all is ok there is no need to search out suffering, practice something else if you are not suffering in the moment, gratitude for example. There will be plenty of opportunities to practice acceptance in the future!

6. *Finding time*

A frequently heard reason for not starting or maintaining a regular mindfulness practice is lack of time. On average we sleep for seven hours and twenty minutes per day. Ten minutes of meditation therefore equals just 1% of our waking day. We can always find time for personal hygiene; people rarely claim that they don't have time for bathing or cleaning their teeth. Mindfulness is hygiene for the mind.

Non-striving vs balanced effort

In the next section we will explore the attitude of non-striving. This does not mean that we do not try but rather that we don't try too hard, not trying to force the outcome. Instead, we approach tasks and challenges with a balanced effort.

Non-striving

"Muddy water is best cleared by leaving it alone." – Alan Watts

We live in a very goal focused world. Much of our lives is target driven, both at work and at home. We are taught from an early age to work hard, to achieve, and try our best. This striving can be positive in some respects as it can help us focus on our goals and achieve them. However, we can get stuck in striving and find ourselves trying too hard in areas of our lives where it just isn't appropriate.

Sometimes when we strive and try too hard, we create tension and lose creativity. If you are learning a new skill such as a musical instrument or learning to drive, quite often, the harder we try, the more mistakes we make because we become tense. If we strive in a creative pursuit, then we may be technically accurate, but the end result may be lacking in some way.

Mindfulness meditation has no goal other than for you to pay attention to the way you are in the moment. Do not grasp for a particular state of mind. Just watch and allow yourself to experience anything and everything from moment to moment. In meditation, when we strive, we create tension and a sense of self criticism. This can get in the way of our practice. In meditation, the more we strive to make something happen, such as trying to relax, the less likely it is to happen. When we practice non-striving in meditation, we might make an effort to focus but we do not force.

The paradox of mindfulness is that often in order for change to take place we need to stay exactly where we are but with awareness and acceptance. Rather than striving to get to the next goal, we learn to understand where we are now.

Non-striving doesn't mean giving up or not trying. Instead, it means making a balanced effort. We are not giving up, but we are not trying too hard either. Instead of having a narrow focus on goal and outcome, we are aware of the process and the journey. We are not striving to get to the top of the mountain - we are enjoying the climb.

The Soft and Hard Edges of Movement

In this lesson, we have already explored the idea of balanced effort - finding the space between giving up on the one hand and trying too hard on the other. We can explore this idea further through mindful movement through finding the space between the soft and hard edges of movement.

In mindful movement, the soft edge is when we can feel the effects of the movement and the hard edge is when it starts to hurt. When we think of exercise and fitness we might think of messages like 'feel the burn' and 'no pain no gain.' These messages encourage striving and, for most of us, can be quite unhelpful. We can be left feeling as though we ought to strive, even though it might not be appropriate for our bodies at that time. Alternatively, we might become frightened of exercise or movement. Perhaps you had a bad experience of sport at school and subsequently tell yourself the story that you can't exercise.

Finding the space between the soft and hard edges of movement takes awareness. We need to learn to listen to our own bodies in order to know what feels right. This might vary from day to day.

Perhaps you attend a gym where there are exercise classes and there is a choice of beginner, intermediate and advanced. Do you automatically attend the beginner class, assuming that you are not good enough to go to intermediate? Or do you force yourself to attend the advanced class even though you are tired and your body wants something more gentle? Or maybe you want to take up running. Can you run past the point of feeling your heart rate rising but stop before you feel sick?

Here are two examples of Mindful movements in which we can explore the soft and hard edges:

Movement One - Raising and Lowering Hands:

- In the first movement either sit with your back straight or stand with your feet hip distance apart.
- Hold your hands in front of you as though you are holding a football.

- Notice your breathing.
- As you breathe in raise your hands upwards and as you breathe out bring your hands back down.
- You may choose to make this a really subtle movement. Alternatively, you might choose to raise your hands right above your head and stretch as you breathe in, and you might choose to fold forward and touch your toes as you breathe out.
- Make the movement as large or as small as feels right for you.

Movement Two – Tree Pose Variation

- Begin standing with your feet together, with your arms at your sides. Bring your attention to your feet and allow a sense of being grounded
- Shift your weight to your left foot. Bend your right knee, then you might choose to lift the right heel so that it rests on the left inner ankle.
- You might choose to lift the right foot so that you are balanced on your left leg. Rest your right foot on the left calf or the left thigh. Do not rest your foot against your knee. Only above or below it.
- Once you have positioned your foot you might choose to bring your hands together in front of you in prayer position. Alternatively, you might choose to raise your hands above your head.
- Once you have chosen your hand position you might choose to close your eyes.

- Hold the posture for as long as feels right for you. You might then repeat on the other side.

In both of the exercises described above, there are several options. Did you automatically choose the most difficult option, or did you play it safe and stay within your comfort zone? Can you apply this tendency to other aspects of your life? What would happen if you applied the principle of the soft and hard edges to your work, your relationships, or your meditation?

Managing Thoughts in Meditation

In meditation, it is normal to become distracted by thoughts. Often intrusive thoughts are the very reason why we decide to practice mindfulness in the first place. We may also find that we are troubled by thoughts at other times throughout the day. Perhaps this comes up when we are trying to sleep or when we are trying to work. This can get in the way of our being present and get in the way of our concentration. The problem with thoughts is that when we try to block them out or push them away, often they come back, louder and stronger. Additionally, when we buy into them, we can find ourselves believing the things that our thoughts are telling us. This can lead to worry and catastrophising. The key, therefore, is to acknowledge thoughts and let them go. The following tools can help us to do this:

1. **Images:**

Some people find that images can be useful in helping to let go of thoughts in meditation. You might imagine that your mind is like the sky and the thoughts are clouds passing by. Or you might imagine the thoughts as leaves on a stream. Come up with your own image to let go of thoughts if that feels helpful. Be as creative as you like! Remember that this is just a tool to manage distraction and is not the meditation itself. Once you have let go of the thought, come back to the focus of the meditation.

2. Body Awareness:

Some thoughts have a greater effect than others and are harder to let go of. These are the thoughts that have an emotional element and trigger an emotional response. Emotional thoughts can have an effect on the body. Becoming aware of this can help us to stay away from the content of the thought and notice what is happening in the moment. For instance, noticing a tightness in the chest when having an anxious thought; rather than getting caught up in the story of the thought and trying to solve it.

3. Noting and Labelling:

Our minds wander, it is what our minds do. When practicing mindfulness, we observe the wandering without getting involved. Previously we have used a focal point, such as the breath, or bodily sensations, to bring our attention back. Simply noticing your thoughts and letting them go is not always as easy as it might seem, and we can find ourselves getting caught up in the content of the thought. It can be helpful to briefly turn the spotlight of our attention to the thought, label it and then let it pass. This can also be extended to include physical sensations and emotions.

In this practice it is useful to keep the label simple and objective, describing the nature of the thought/sensation or feeling rather than the content. Mindful awareness is knowing what is happening as it is happening. Through labelling we bring our awareness to what is on our mind moment by moment. You might label a thought as 'planning' or 'fantasy', a physical sensation as sound or pain, an emotion as anger or shame and then let it go. Practicing in this way we can become more aware of our habitual thought patterns and create the space to break the cycle of rumination.

Labelling practice

The practice of labelling can be used as part of any meditation or as a practice in its own right. As with other practices we have a primary focal point to anchor our attention, the breath, physical sensations etc, however we also have a secondary focus on whatever else arises. In the labelling practice we give a simple one word label to the secondary stimuli as it arises in our attention. This can be practiced sitting or lying down or as part of mindful movement practice.

- Start by finding a comfortable relaxed but alert meditation position of your choice.
- Take a few moments to settle into your posture allowing a sense of feeling grounded.
- Choose a primary focus for your attention. In this example we shall be using the breath.

- Bring your attention to the breath. Breathing in you are aware that you are breathing in, breathing out you are aware that you are breathing out.
- Before long you will become aware of secondary stimuli, such as thoughts, physical sensations or emotions.
- Whatever arises, give it a descriptive label, a simple neutral word. Initially you may wish to start with a broad label – such as 'thinking', 'sound', or 'physical sensation'. Or you may wish to provide a more descriptive label of the nature of the stimulus – such as 'planning', 'a ticking clock', 'tingling'.
- Once you have acknowledged and labelled the event, gently return to the anchor of the breath.
- Rest in the support of the breath patiently waiting for the next thing to arise, not looking for anything and being curious about what will arise next.
- Repeat this process over and over again. Notice, label, return to the breath, notice, label return to the breath.
- Notice the tone and attitude of your labelling. Try to bring a non-judgemental kindly acceptance to whatever arises. If you are alone you may wish to say the label out loud, further reinforcing the acknowledgement of whatever is there or just mentally apply the label in your mind.
- When you are ready, let go of the labelling, open your eyes if they have been closed and bring the practice to a close.

If you wish, you can record in your journal what you noticed, just list the labels you applied in the session that you can recall.

Over time these journal entries can bring insight to your default patterns.

Whenever we notice thoughts in meditation, the key is to observe with curiosity rather than beating yourself up and telling yourself you are failing. Every time you notice a thought, this is a moment of awareness. Every moment of awareness in our meditation *is* the meditation.

The Mindfulness of Breathing

The mindfulness of breathing is a meditation that enables us to develop deeper concentration and focus. Practising this meditation regularly can help us to develop the skills to manage our thoughts. We are not trying to empty the mind. We are not trying to get rid of thoughts. We are observing what happens when we become distracted and returning our attention to the breath.

In the mindfulness of breathing, we simply follow and observe the felt sensations of the breath. Try using some of the methods described above to manage thoughts in meditation

You don't need to breathe in any particular way. What is important is to be aware of how the breath is moment by moment. When we are aware of the breath we are in the moment.

Settling and Grounding

- Find yourself a comfortable relaxed meditation posture. If you are sitting on a chair, then sitting with your feet flat on the floor and with your back upright following the spine's natural curve. The body is relaxed but with a sense of poise and alertness. If it is more appropriate for your body to practice lying or in another posture of your choice, then this is absolutely fine. Lightly close your eyes if that feels appropriate for you.

- Connect with a sense of being grounded. This might mean noticing the felt sensations of the ground beneath your feet or the contact you can feel with your chair, or whatever you are sitting on.
- When you are ready turn your attention to the felt sensations of the breath.

Stage One

- In the first stage we use counting to support our focus on the breath. Follow the breath in and follow the breath out, silently saying a number after the end of each out-breath.
- Breathe in, breathe out, 'one', breathe in, breathe out, 'two', and so on up to ten and then begin again from one.
- Allow the counting to be light and your main focus to be on the felt sensations of breathing.
- If you become distracted, bring your attention back to the breath and begin again from one.
- Remember it is normal to become distracted!

Stage Two

- In the second stage you anticipate the breath by counting before the in-breath.
- 'One', breathe in, breathe out, 'two', breathe in, breathe out, and so on up to ten and then beginning again from one.
- If you become distracted, bring your attention back to the breath and begin again from one.
- You may only ever count up to two or three and that is absolutely fine. Every time you notice that you are distracted is a moment of awareness so congratulate yourself for noticing and bring yourself back.

Ending

- When you are ready let go of the counting and just watch the breath. Come back to a sense of being grounded. In your own time let go of any effort, open your eyes, and bring the meditation to a close

Rachel's Story: A musical meditation

I have been playing the saxophone for around five years and my experience of learning a new instrument is that I have also learned the value of non-striving.

I had my first lesson at the age of 32. You are never too old to learn a new skill after all. In my first lesson I managed to set up the saxophone and blow into it and make a squeaky sound. In my second lesson I produced my first note! It was a triumph! I steadily improved. I learned to read music and I found something just for me. Here I found something that isn't about work. It isn't about getting up on stage. It is about pure enjoyment. It is learning for the sake of learning and playing for the sheer joy of it.

But because it has no purpose other than itself, I can often talk myself out of playing. Why is it that I still believe work is more important than play? This is part of striving. I have spent much of my life being a self-confessed workaholic, rarely doing anything if it couldn't link back to work in some way.

So I often find myself trying to think of excuses not to play. I'm not in the mood. I have too much on my mind. Maybe I should do something more productive. What if it disturbs the neighbours? What if it upsets the cat? I can do it later! My saxophone sits waiting to be played. I love playing and yet so often I can't bring myself to do it.

As I play my first note, my cat, Sheema, raises her head from where she had been sleeping in a sunbeam. She looks at me with a mixture of horror and disgust and skulks away, finding somewhere as far away from earshot as possible. Everyone's a critic! And yet once that first note has been played nothing else matters.

Half an hour later and I am engrossed. It turns out that it is very difficult to read music and move my fingers in the right way and move my mouth in the right way and worry at the same time. As I play, my mind becomes still.

I have been a meditator for around 20 years, and I have taught mindfulness and meditation for around 14 years. So it turns out that

I have found myself a musical meditation. By focusing on my hands, my mouth, and the music I quieten the mental chatter.

In practicing the saxophone, I am also practicing the attitude of non-striving. The harder I try to get it perfect, the more likely I am to squeak horribly or make a simple mistake. Instead of over-thinking the perfect execution of a piece I trust that my fingers know what they are doing. When I let go of striving, I am less likely to stumble - I am also less likely to beat myself up.

In playing the saxophone I have learned to enjoy an activity for its own sake. I have learned that it is ok not to be productive all the time. I have learned that time spent joyfully playing music, however imperfectly, is time well spent. My cat still doesn't like it though!

Summary

When we try too hard or strive, we create tension. This can lead to mistakes or a lack of creativity. Non-striving means making a balanced effort. We still try but this effort is not strained or forced.

We can practice balanced effort through the practice of mindful movement. In some exercises we can find the gap between the soft and hard edge of a movement. The soft edge is when we can first feel the movement and the hard edge is when it starts to hurt. Some of us have a tendency to push ourselves too hard while others might find that we stay in our comfort zone and don't push ourselves enough! By seeking out the space between the hard and soft edges in movement we can learn to practice non-striving in everyday life.

Many people strive in meditation, believing that they need

to empty their minds. In doing so, we fight against thoughts and create tension and a sense of failure. When we practice a mindful meditation, we are not trying to get rid of thoughts. Instead, we are learning to relate to them differently. We learn to acknowledge thoughts and let them go. There are several ways to manage thoughts. We might use images; we might use body awareness; we might use labelling. What is important is that we do not try to force the thought out, but we also try not to get too caught up with it.

The mindfulness of breathing uses counting to help us to focus on the breath. This meditation can help in the development of focus and concentration. While we will never empty the mind, using the breath as an anchor can help to settle and quieten the mind.

Home practice

This week, see if you can practice a mindfulness of breathing meditation each day. As you practice the meditation, you might explore the different methods of working with thoughts that we have explored in this lesson. You might find that one method is more effective with certain types of thoughts while another method is more effective with other types of thoughts.

Also this week, see if you can practice some mindful movement each day and explore the space between the soft and hard edges. You might also apply this principle to other physical activity such as an exercise class or a trip to the gym.

As always, make a note of your observations in your journal.

Questions for Reflection

Q1. Do you find that you are more likely to try too hard or not hard enough?

Q2. What does striving feel like? Does it feel different to non-striving?

lesson six: letting go

This lesson's attitude is letting go. We spend much of our time clinging onto things that simply do not serve us. This might be habits, beliefs, or unpleasant memories. When we practise letting go, we allow our experience to change in its own time. We can practice this in meditation through the mindfulness of sounds and thoughts practice. We notice sounds and we let them go. We notice thoughts and we let them go. There is nothing to fix or change and there is no point in trying to cling on because our experience will change anyway!

In this lesson we introduce a simple meditation called the three-minute breathing space, in which we tune into our experience of the present moment; we tune into the breath; and we tune into our surroundings - all in only three minutes! This is an excellent practice to use to punctuate your day.

Home Practice Review: Further reflections on finding balance

In the previous lesson we explored the attitude of non-striving in relation to mindful movement and a breathing meditation. Our aim in these practices is to practice balanced effort and find the gap between the hard and soft edges. We are making some effort, but we are not straining or forcing. The problem arises when we start to strive to find perfect balance! This is an impossible task. We are always trying too hard or not hard enough in pretty much any task we are performing. The aim is not to find perfect balance but to notice the imbalance and calibrate. For example, you might notice that you are becoming tense and choose to calibrate so that you are not trying so hard. And then you might notice that your practice has become a little vague and choose to calibrate so that you are making a little more effort.

When it comes to mindful movement, you may have noticed that you have a different experience when you are practising alone compared with when practising in a group. It might be worth noticing whether you push yourself harder when there are other people around to compete with!

This lesson's attitude is letting go. And this might be a welcome attitude - reminding us to let go of our perfectionism and our need to get it right!

Letting Go

When I let go of what I am, I become what I might be. When I let go of what I have, I receive what I need. Lao Tzu

When we practice letting go, we cultivate non-attachment. We let go of the I, me, and mine.

Neuroscientists call our tendency to self-reference our experience as the default mode network. This is the tendency to interpret and judge events in terms of their impact on us: 'I like this'; 'I don't like this'; 'this is irrelevant to me'. This leads to habitual patterns of behaviour that may no longer serve us. When we start paying attention to our inner experience, we discover thoughts and feelings we like and want to hold on to, thoughts and feelings we dislike and want to push away and thoughts, feelings and sensations that seem irrelevant and we often choose to ignore.

Sometimes we cling on to what is familiar, even if it is unpleasant. By letting go we accept that change is inevitable. In doing so we embrace the reality of change rather than fighting against it. By clinging on, pushing away, and resisting change we are ignoring the reality that we have very little control of external circumstances. We only ever really have control over how we respond in this moment. Letting go is the acceptance of reality.

When we practice letting go, we let go of the tendency to grasp and push away. In doing so we create space to allow the next thought, feeling or sensation to arise.

When we practice mindfulness, we practice being in the present moment. However, our minds will often take us into memories of the past or speculation about the future. When we let go, we are not letting go of memories or prior learning, but we are letting go of the tendency to ruminate, glorify the past or constantly replay alternate scenarios of something that has already passed. 'If only I had done that', 'If only I had said this' etc. Nor are we letting go of hopes or aspirations. It does not mean we cannot make plans. However, we are practicing letting go of the tendency to catastrophise and letting go of attachment to outcome. When we become attached to an outcome that that does not materialise, we can become overwhelmed by feelings of failure and unworthiness.

Our intentions provide a direction of travel. Meditation brings our awareness to where we are on the journey. There is no specific destination in mind. When we let go of attachment to outcome, we accept things as they are rather than how we think things are supposed to be.

When practising letting go in meditation, we let things go, both pleasant and unpleasant, and we just watch. We notice pleasant experiences arise, change and fade and we notice unpleasant experiences arise, change and fade without clinging to either and without pushing anything away.

If we find it particularly difficult to let go of something because it has such a strong hold on our mind, we can direct our attention to what 'holding' feels like. Holding on is the opposite of letting go. Being willing to look at the ways we hold shows a lot about its opposite.

We notice thoughts as they arise and let them go by returning to our chosen focus – the breath, physical sensations, sounds etc. This does not mean suppressing thoughts, it is bringing awareness to them and letting them go.

You already know how to let go; with every new breath we breathe, we let go to enable the next.

Mark's Story: Letting Go of Who I Thought I Was Supposed To Be

On 30th June 2010 I chaired the SITRA National Homelessness conference; the role of chair was by invitation. On the face of it I was at the height of my career, a nationally recognized expert in my field. It was also the day my career in homelessness effectively ended, it was the day of my redundancy from my employer. My role as Director of Operations was essentially that of Deputy Chief Executive. Unfortunately, after five years of an effective and trusting relationship with the Chief Executive, the previous year had seen a deterioration in our relationship culminating in an agreement for me to take voluntary redundancy. A decent financial package was agreed along with a non-disclosure agreement.

I walked to the train station with one of the delegates, a senior civil servant in the Department of Communities and Local Government. I mentioned my redundancy and expressed my uncertainty over my future direction. I still remember his words clearly "Please stay in homelessness, the sector needs leaders like you" These were lovely words to hear, and I assured him that it was my intention, it was part of my identity.

I had been working for the leading homelessness organisation in the region and had previously worked for most of the rest. After three months of job applications and interviews it became clear that the only way I could stay in the sector was to relocate. It was clear that locally I was considered over-qualified for the available roles and there was a level of distrust compounded by the non-disclosure agreement that limited what I could say about why I had left such a significant role voluntarily. However, I was settled in the region. My wife had a good job, and my children were at a crucial stage in their education.

I was angry, this was not the way things were supposed to be!

I chose to stay and enrolled on a leadership and performance coaching qualification at the local university. If I couldn't be a leader in the sector, maybe I could help develop leaders in the sector. The course was part time and shortly after starting I was offered and accepted a temporary contract to manage a Drug and Alcohol Rehabilitation project. Not quite the same sector, but close enough, I was again doing what I knew. Six months later I accepted the role on a permanent basis. On 30th June 2012 I was again made redundant. Changes in treatment and funding resulted in the closure of many residential rehabilitation projects, including the one I managed.

I was angry, this was not the way things were supposed to be!

I was stuck, I didn't know what to do, I blamed individuals, organisations, and the system. It wasn't my fault, and it was unfair. There were periods of deep despair I no longer had a clear identity. I had the support of a loving family and some close friends, I was a husband, a father, and a friend but it didn't seem like enough. I desperately searched for a new identity, I tried working as a sales director for a video production company, set up a charity promoting peace, returned briefly to a lesser role in the homelessness sector and even considered opening a gourmet hot dog franchise! I didn't know who I was anymore, and nor did those around me. My relationships suffered; something had to change, or I would lose everything.

I was angry, this was not the way things were supposed to be!

In tandem to all this chaos I was developing my mindfulness practice. Initially, mindfulness offered me brief moments of peace and calm. As my practice deepened there came insight. I discovered liberation through the foundational attitudes and in particular, I learned to let go. I started by letting go of my anger and resentment to others, I let go of the need to find blame. I took responsibility and let go of the illusion of control of external circumstances. And finally, I let go of the idea that things were supposed to be a particular way for me. By letting go of who I thought I was supposed to be I discovered the freedom and happiness of being who I have become.

The Three-Minute Breathing Space

The three-minute breathing space provides an excellent opportunity to practice letting go. We need to let go of each out-breath to welcome in the next in-breath. This is a simple meditation that provides an opportunity to reconnect with yourself and become aware of how you are. We begin with a broad sense of how we are right now; we then move on to observe the breath; and finally, we broaden out our awareness to observe the sounds around us. Generally, each part of the meditation lasts a minute, but you can spend as long as you like on each stage. You can practice in your normal meditation posture if you wish. However, you might also choose to practice at your desk at work, or even in the queue at the supermarket!

- Find yourself a comfortable position for this practice. You may choose a formal meditation posture with your eyes closed. Or you may choose to straighten your back slightly wherever you are – standing, sitting, or lying. Only close your eyes if it is safe and appropriate to do so!

- When you are ready start with a broad sense of yourself. You might notice sensations in your body. You might notice your emotions. You might notice if your mind is busy or still. There is nothing to fix or change. Just notice how things are in the moment.

- Then turn your attention to your breath. Notice how it feels as you breathe in and out. Again, there is nothing to fix; there is nothing to change. Simply observe the breath.

- Finally, broaden your attention to observe the sounds around you. You might notice the sounds nearest to you as well as the furthest away. Some sounds you might like, and some sounds you might not like. Just notice. And then when you're ready bring the meditation to a close.

Mindfulness and Choice

In Buddhism there is the story of the second arrow. This story tells of the difference between a wise person and an unwise person in response to suffering. When a wise person is shot by an arrow it hurts. They remove the arrow and then it is over. When the unwise person is shot by an arrow it still hurts but then they get caught up in anger and blame and trying to figure out who shot them and why and plotting revenge! For this person it is like shooting themselves with a second arrow. The wise person experiences pain but chooses not to add to it. The unwise person experiences pain and adds further suffering.

So how does this apply to you? Imagine you are running late for an important meeting, and you are stuck in traffic? You might experience some anxiety? You might notice feeling nauseous or you might notice your heart rate increasing? This is like the first arrow. This is our immediate, often unavoidable response, to suffering or stress. However, quite often we also add to our suffering. We beat ourselves up - telling ourselves how stupid we are and how we should have taken a different route or left the house earlier. Or maybe we catastrophise, telling ourselves all the things that will go wrong if we are late for our meeting. We practice a kind of mental time travel where we project ourselves into the future and that future is generally not good. Perhaps we distract ourselves from our anxiety by smoking or drinking or starting an argument with someone. All of these reactions are like shooting ourselves with a second arrow - or even a second, third and fourth arrow! We can't control traffic. We can't control our initial physical or emotional response to the things that happen to us. But we can choose to let go of our reactions. We can choose not to add the second arrow.

Mindfulness helps us to distinguish between the first and second arrows. Mindfulness helps us to know what to accept and what to let go of.

Mindfulness of Sounds and thoughts

Sounds are everywhere. We are surrounded by a soundscape. Sometimes we can regard sound as a distraction in meditation. However, we can make sound the focus of our meditation. What was distraction from meditation can *become* the meditation. Additionally, working with sound in meditation can also help us to work with thoughts in meditation. Just as we cannot block out thoughts, we cannot block out sound. In any moment there are sounds: the sounds of our body, our breathing, and sounds from the external world. Awareness of the nature of sounds can help us develop a greater understanding of the nature of thoughts.

Sounds and thoughts share many things in common. Like thoughts, sounds are generally self-arising - they just appear. We can, of course, make a sound happen, just like we can choose to think about something, but pretty soon other sounds will also appear. Sounds are self-liberating - they come and they go and, like thoughts, they are constantly changing.

We constantly judge sounds: 'I like that,' 'I want that to stop', 'it's just irrelevant in the background'. We have a tendency to attach meaning to the content of sound, to identify it and make sense of why it is there. Sounds can evoke memories and emotions.

Mindfulness of sounds involves bringing your awareness to the soundscape. Allowing sounds to arise and treating them simply as sounds. Focusing on the nature of the symphony of sounds available in each moment without following them or listening out for anything in particular. Tuning in to the nature of the sound rather than the content, noticing pitch, volume, tone etc. Bringing awareness to any emotions that arise or the tendency to label and attach meaning then letting go and allowing the next sound to arise.

The following practice begins with mindfulness of sounds and then we shift our attention from the soundscape to the 'thoughtscape', relating to thoughts in the same way.

Mindfulness of Sounds and Thoughts Meditation

- Start by finding a comfortable, relaxed, and alert posture, embodying the intention to meditate. Close your eyes or, if you prefer, soften the focus on a neutral point in front of you.
- Notice the points of contact with the surfaces supporting you, letting go of any sense of holding and allowing a sense of being grounded, held and supported by the ground beneath you.
- Gently turn your attention to the breath. Spend a few moments bringing your awareness to the sensations of the breath.
- Sharpen your focus to sounds of the breath and broaden this awareness to the sounds that surround you.
- As each sound arises see if you can let go of the habit of naming and judging it. Try not to follow sounds, just allow them to come to you. Allow yourself to bathe in the soundscape!
- If a particular sound begins to grab your attention, gently redirect your focus to any other sounds that are available in your soundscape

- If your mind begins to wander, kindly guide it back to the symphony of sounds available to you.
- Now gently returning the focus of attention to the breath, resting in the support of the breath.
- As thoughts arise gently turn your attention to your thoughtscape. Try and experience thoughts just as mental processes arising like sounds in the mind.
- Notice how thoughts, like sounds, randomly appear. Allow the ever-changing thoughtscape to be the focus of your practice right now.
- There is no need to control them, change them or fix them, just allow them to come and go, listening to the playlist of your mind.
- If your thoughts become overwhelming gently come back to the breath for a few moments before gently returning to the thoughtscape.
- Now slowly open up to the space around you, notice the sounds inside and outside the room as you bring this practice to a close.

Just Sitting

In the Just Sitting Practice we have another opportunity to practice letting go. We notice the experiences that come into our awareness, and we let them go, without pushing away or getting too caught up. We begin by noticing the breath. We then notice felt sensations in the body. We then move onto observe emotions. We then notice thoughts and then sounds as they come and go. We then just sit. We just sit and notice whatever comes to our awareness moment-by-moment. We are not trying to focus on anything in particular. We simply notice whatever emerges and then let it go.

- Find yourself a comfortable meditation posture. Lightly close your eyes if that feels comfortable for you. Connect with a sense of being grounded.
- Bring your attention to your breath. Just notice the changing sensations of breathing. Letting go of the out-breath and welcoming in the next in-breath. Each breath a letting go.
- Bring your attention to felt sensations in the body. You might notice pleasant sensations. You might notice unpleasant sensations. Just observe and let go. You might notice how sensations change moment by moment.
- Bring your attention to your emotions. You might be aware of strong emotions or subtle emotions. You might not know what emotions you are feeling. We are not trying to change anything or make anything happen. We are simply observing and letting go.
- Bring your attention to thoughts. Notice if your mind is busy or still. See if you can observe each thought and let it pass.
- Notice the sounds around you. Some loud, some quiet, some pleasant, some unpleasant. Allow the sounds to come and go moment by moment.
- For the last few minutes of this practice, we simply sit. Notice whatever comes to your attention. You might notice thoughts, sounds, emotions, felt sensations. Just notice whatever you notice. Notice how your experience

changes moment by moment. And whatever you notice, let it go.

Whenever you are ready open your eyes and bring the practice to a close.

Summary

We spend much of our time clinging onto beliefs, habits, and experiences - both pleasant and unpleasant. And this often causes us suffering. The attitude of letting go is the antidote to this and is a reminder that change is inevitable, whether we like it or not.

The three-minute breathing space is a simple opportunity to check in with yourself and can be practised any time.

Often when we experience something unpleasant, rather than letting go, we add to our own suffering. We do this through our thoughts and our behaviour. We often have very little choice about the things that happen in life and we don't have a choice about our immediate physiological and emotional responses but we do have a choice about what to do next.

Mindfulness of sounds and thoughts is another opportunity to practice letting go. Sounds come and go. Thoughts come and go. We simply observe and let go without getting caught up.

Finally, the just sitting practice provides the opportunity to take a step back and notice whatever comes into your awareness. You are not actively focusing on anything in particular - but bringing a receptive awareness to whatever emerges.

Home Practice

This week see if you can practice a mindfulness of sounds and thoughts meditation each day. Notice how it feels to observe and let go. You might find that some sounds are easier to let go of than others and some thoughts are easier to let go of than others. Make a note of your observations in your journal. Also, this week see if you can practice the three-minute breathing space. You might choose this practice on days when you feel that you don't have time for a longer meditation. Alternatively, you might choose to add in the three-minute breathing space throughout your day. It is an excellent practice to try during TV ad breaks or in between meetings at work.

Finally see if you can spend a couple of minutes just sitting, without focusing your attention on anything in particular. You might do this as a stand-alone meditation, or you might choose to end a more formal meditation practice with five minutes of just sitting.

Questions for Reflection

Q1. Do you find that you are more likely to cling onto things that you like or things that you don't like?

Q2. What gets in the way of letting go?

Q3. How does it feel when you let go?

lesson seven: generosity

This lesson's attitude is generosity. This does not mean self-sacrifice or giving away all of our worldly possessions. In fact, sometimes the most generous gift we can give is the gift of our own attention. In this lesson we will explore the attitude of generosity and the practice of kindness both in relation to others and in relation to ourselves. And we will also be introducing a new meditation. In the kindness meditation we actively direct our minds towards generating kind thoughts and feelings towards ourselves and others. This includes people that we don't like and, as such, can be quite a radical practice! In this lesson we will also explore some of the neuroscience behind our emotions and how the practices of mindfulness, kindness and compassion can help to regulate our emotions.

Home Practice Review: Letting Go in Practice

In the previous lesson we introduced a short breathing practice that we can do throughout the day at any time. This can be particularly helpful in moments of stress or anxiety. However, sometimes we might feel too overwhelmed to be able to access the practice. The 3-minute breathing space is often used in moments of stress to enable us to take a break and let go. However, it might not be wise to wait until we are stressed to practice it. If your stress levels have become acute then you are less likely to remember to practice a mindfulness exercise and you might find it more challenging. Instead, you might notice the very early warning signs that you are becoming stressed and do it then, or just choose a time each day to practice. You might even practice it 2 or 3 times each day - it is only three minutes after all!

In the previous lesson we explored the attitude of letting go in relation to sounds and thoughts. Sometimes it can be difficult to let go of thoughts if they seem too important or if they feel particularly distressing. If you have a thought during meditation that you feel is really important and you are scared you might forget it, you might choose to have a little notebook next to you when you are meditating. Write down the thought as succinctly as possible and then let it go and return to the meditation. However, in time hopefully you can learn to trust that if the thought is important enough it will return! We don't have very many original thoughts anyway!

If you notice that the thought is distressing, you might anchor yourself by focusing on your breath or by noticing sensations of being grounded. Bring your attention to the feet on the floor or your bottom on your chair. You might notice the feelings of being distressed in your body, rather than getting caught up on the content of the thought or trying to solve it. However, it might be that the meditation has brought up something that needs to be addressed. It might be helpful to seek out a friend or a professional to talk to about your thoughts and feelings.

Sometimes it can feel that letting go is just too hard! There are lots of reasons for this. Change can be scary. We might prefer the familiar even if it is unpleasant. Remind yourself that it is normal to be afraid. We might hold onto resentment towards others because we believe that they have wronged us and they deserve our anger. However, when we let go, we do so because we deserve peace, not because they deserve forgiveness! This lesson's attitude is Generosity. Perhaps you could think of forgiveness as an act of generosity towards yourself.

Generosity

'Attention is the Rarest and Purest form of Generosity'
Simone Weil

There are many ways to practice generosity, both towards ourselves and towards others. And yet generosity can feel challenging. We may feel that we don't have the time or the resources to be generous. We might worry about how our generosity may be perceived. We may shy away from being kind to ourselves because we don't feel worthy. And often we simply don't recognise the many ways that we are already generous.

Generosity may mean giving something materially. Equally, it could be giving our time, our knowledge and expertise, our attention, or our help. Giving a smile can be a huge act of generosity! When we share pleasant experiences with others it can sometimes be hard to know who is being generous to whom. Sometimes accepting a gift and allowing someone else's generosity can be a generous act. After all we all appreciate the opportunity to be kind. True generosity is not about giver or receiver but about connection.

Meditation can be an act of generosity towards ourselves, giving ourselves time to pay ourselves attention. And when this begins to impact positively on those around us, our mindfulness practice can be an act of generosity towards the world!

Rachel's Story: 5 Questions to End Your Day

How do you end your day? Maybe you end your day by watching TV or scrolling through social media. Or maybe you spend your evening looking back over your day at everything that has gone wrong? Or maybe you continue working until you flop into bed, exhausted?

None of these things feel good! Now this isn't a moment to beat yourself up — I know that I do all of those things at some point! And I also know that it doesn't serve me.
I have recently started a new practice that I like to end my day with. My friends often buy me journals for Christmas and birthdays, and I often leave them empty — thinking that I have nothing good enough to write. Now I have! So, I invite you to grab yourself a journal and on the first page write the following five questions:

1. *What am I grateful for today?*

2. *What am I proud of today?*

3. *What have I learned today?*

4. *What made me laugh today?*

5. *How was I generous today?*

Each day before I go to bed, I take a few minutes to reflect on these questions and write down my responses. They do not need to be huge. This is a moment to reflect on the simple things and to pay ourselves generous attention. Here's some examples of the kinds of things that I write.

1. ***What am I grateful for today?*** *I am always grateful for my cat. She makes me smile and she is very affectionate. I am also grateful for nature, having been on a walk and spotted*

some beautiful wild daisies. When I practice gratitude, which we introduced in lesson three, it gives me a sense of abundance, which helps me to practice generosity. As we learn more about the attitudes we start to see how they each link to one another.

1. **What am I proud of today?** I sometimes describe this as my little wins. This could include doing some DIY that I had been putting off for a while. I now have a picture up on my wall rather than lingering on my to-do list!

2. **What have I learned today?** Now this one could be a life lesson or an interesting fact or a new skill. It might even be something that we learned from making a mistake! I have learned that it is a good idea to label food before putting it in the freezer – and at the same time discovered a new meal – bolognaise tacos!

3. **What made me laugh today?** This might be a TV programme, a moment with friends, a podcast or just a silly idea that came to me. It is so easy to forget those little humorous moments. As I am recording this I am reminded of a moment I shared with my co-author, Mark earlier today. We were having a serious conversation and I then made him laugh with a very rude comment. And his laughter made me laugh. I'm not sharing the joke!

4. **How was I generous today?** As we have already explored, we are generous all the time and often don't even realise it. Sometimes my act of generosity is making a donation to a food bank. But it doesn't need to be a material gift. A smile, a text message or a kind word. And self-kindness counts too!

Try it yourself. Write down your answers to these five questions every evening before bed and notice how you feel. Paying attention to yourself in asking yourself these questions is an act of generosity.

Memories of Generosity Meditation

In this meditation we reflect on acts of generosity that we have received, performed, and witnessed. In lesson three we discussed negativity bias – our tendency to focus on the negative – and how this can be challenged through the practice of generosity. In a similar way, the memories of generosity meditation can challenge our negativity bias in relation to ourselves and others. We practice focusing on moments of generosity rather than selfishness.

- Find a comfortable sitting posture and close your eyes if that is comfortable for you.
- Recall a time when someone was generous to you. You may have received a gift, maybe someone helped you in some way or just listened to you. It doesn't need to be something huge - just a simple act of kindness. Notice how you feel when you bring it to mind. Try and recall this act of generosity in as much detail as you can. Recall who was there, what you were wearing, the time of day, where you were, any sounds - replay this moment in your mind's eye. Notice if you can recall how you felt at the time and notice how you feel now as you recall receiving kindness from another.
- Recall a time when you were kind or generous to someone else. Notice how you feel when you recall giving to

another. Again, try and recall in as much detail as you can this act of generosity. Recall who was there, what you were wearing, the time of day, where you were, any sounds - replay this moment in your mind's eye. Notice if you can recall how you felt at the time and notice how you feel now as you recall an act of giving to another.

- Now see if you can recall a time when you witnessed or heard about the generosity of others. This might be something you have witnessed in work, or even on the news or social media. Notice how it feels to bring this to mind. Notice how it feels to connect with generosity, even if you are not directly involved.

- You might also recall a time when you were generous towards yourself, connecting with your own capacity to practice self-care.

- Notice how it feels to recall and reflect upon all of these different forms of generosity.

- When you are ready, let go of the practice. Notice the sounds around you and open your eyes, bringing the meditation to a close.

The Emotion Regulation Systems

Our brain has evolved over many thousands of years and has become increasingly complex to overcome the changing challenges in the world. This has resulted in human beings becoming the most dominant species on the planet. However, physical and mental evolution is a very slow process compared to the evolution of societies and infra-structures. Internal systems that evolved to help us deal with the challenges we faced 50,000 years ago still remain. However, they are not always as useful in the modern world.

This evolved brain is continually monitoring physical, sensory, and cognitive information and creates emotional reactions based on sub-conscious interpretation of the data it receives. The human brain is a magnificent super-computer and time machine! It can take us into the future, with varying degrees of accuracy. It can take us into a version of the past, often triggering physical and emotional responses as if it was happening now and it can fill in the gaps to make sense of the present – again with varying degrees of accuracy.

All of this can be incredibly useful. Unfortunately, it can also be agonisingly

unhelpful. Together they brought us to where we are today. Our imagination has resulted in countless inventions from basic tools to the internet. Our ability to learn from the past has enabled us to pass on knowledge to subsequent

generations. Our ability to make sense of what is happening helped us master fire, develop agriculture and much more. However, on an individual basis our negativity bias and tendency to judge can produce less positive results, often creating unwanted anxieties about the future.

Hollywood movies set in the future tend to portray a very negative view of progress. How many futuristic films portray a safer, more connected, and happier world? Likewise, our negative memories can trigger negative judgements and lead to us replaying and reliving trauma. Our need to make sense of what is going on is only useful when we *can* make sense of it. However, if we can't, our inner critic will chip in with self-judgements such as 'I'm not good enough,' 'I'm stupid,' etc. Imposter syndrome is a natural and direct consequence of negativity bias and a perceived lack of a piece of knowledge or skill.

The model of the emotional regulation systems developed by Paul Gilbert can help us to understand how our mind works and, with awareness, choose our responses and rewire our brains. This model applies to us all. However, experiential and developmental factors impact on how these systems function from individual to individual.

The model identifies three separate, but interlinked elements to the emotional regulation systems:

The Threat and Drive systems are connected to the sympathetic nervous system and the Soothe system connected to the para sympathetic nervous system.

Importantly, in terms of self-regulation, it is not possible for the sympathetic and parasympathetic nervous system to operate at the same time.

Sixty thousand years ago we would leave our camp where we felt safe and secure with our tribe (Soothe system) to find food (Drive system). We were aware other creatures, often bigger, stronger and faster were also looking for food (Threat system). We would then return to camp (Soothe system). This simple system continues to direct our behaviour to this day.

However, the threats are different - for most of us most of the time they are

not life threatening. The rewards are different. There are now so many things

we need to do, and must get, but few are essential to survival. Whilst connection and belonging remain essentially the same, the complexities of modern society lead to greater isolation and feelings of loneliness.

The Threat System

Primarily controlled by one of the oldest parts of the brain, the amygdala, the Threat system is our survival instinct. Often referred to as the fight, flight or freeze system it developed to simply notice danger and keep us alive. Likened to a lizard, it is constantly alert and ready to react in an instant. It is so good we often react to danger even before the threat enters our conscious awareness. We inherited such a sensitive amygdala from our ancestors. Those that were hyper-alert to danger survived and passed on their genes. Those that admired the pretty stripes and shiny teeth approaching them didn't!

When we sense danger, the amygdala signals the body to produce cortisol and adrenaline. We breathe faster shallower breaths, taking in oxygen to the blood stream. Our heart beats faster pumping blood to the arms and legs. The cortisol gives additional strength for speed and power. Our awareness focusses on our eyes and ears; we become aware of every sound and can see where to run or hit. Our immune system shuts down and in extreme cases our digestive system will evacuate. Our body is prioritizing what is needed for survival. Infection and hunger are the least of our problems when facing imminent death.

This was great when the threat was a bear or tiger and still useful now when a speeding car is hurtling towards you when you are crossing the road. However, most of the perceived threats in the modern world are rarely immediately life threatening, but our amygdala does not differentiate between real, psychological or imagined threat. Horror movies would be pointless if it did! Nor does it distinguish between internal and external threats, our inner critic can trigger the same reaction. Unfortunately, our neuro-physical response to threat is rarely useful in the face of modern day to day threats. Throwing the computer across the room or punching the boss is unlikely to result in a positive resolution to the impending deadline on a report.

The activated Threat system triggers fear, stress, and anxiety. The deactivated or default mode generates feelings of safety and security. Awareness of the nature of the threat can help us to switch back to the default mode.

Practising generosity shifts our focus from ourselves to others, from what we have, to what we can give. Studies have shown that giving, time or money, reduces activity in the amygdala thus reducing stress and anxiety (Inagaki and Ross 2018).

The Drive System

Primarily controlled by the next part of the brain to evolve, the nuclus accumbens, the Drive system focuses on reward. Likened to a mouse, it is constantly scurrying around looking for the next tasty morsel. It is all about getting things done. It seeks opportunities to achieve goals and secure resources.

This is our doing mode; it is all about doing, earning, having, and winning more. When we achieve something we want or believe we need, the powerful hormone dopamine is produced. Dopamine feels great; we get a buzz from getting stuff we want, winning stuff, securing a promotion etc. However, the high doesn't tend to last very long and off we go seeking the next thing, the next dopamine hit and repeat. Our drive system gives us the focus to complete tasks, learn new skills and achieve goals. It can also lead to addictive and compulsive behaviours, often shutting out our friends and loved ones in the pursuit of success. Failure to succeed can easily lead to self-criticism and a return to threat mode.

The activated Drive system generates feelings of wanting, needing, lack. The deactivated mode encourages feelings of contentment, abundance and satisfaction. Practising gratitude can bring appreciation to what we already have and practicing generosity often leads to receiving more.

Generosity activates our Drive system; generosity is rewarding because it makes us feel good about ourselves and the recipient of our kindness. It also has a ripple effect. When we witness kindness we are more likely to be kind; when others witness our generosity they too are more likely to be generous.

The Soothe System

Primarily controlled by the most recent part of the brain to evolve, the Prefrontal cortex, the soothe system focuses on rest, repair, and connection. Likened to a monkey, it is curious, caring, and social. It is all about connection, contentment, and peace. It promotes healing, growth, belonging and trust.

This is our being mode. It is about non-doing, non-striving, kindness, caring and loving. The Soothe system manages distress and promotes bonding. Chemicals produced by the Soothe system include oxytocin and serotonin. Sometimes referred to as the cuddle or relationship hormone, oxytocin is also produced though physical contact – the more loving the relationship, the greater the production of oxytocin.

Any parents reading this book will probably be aware of the importance of oxytocin in bonding and attachment for newborns. It is a naturally produced sedative and pain killer.

Serotonin, sometimes called the happy hormone, stabilises our mood, promoting feelings of well-being and happiness. It also promotes sleep and digestion. Many anti-depressants are called SSRI's or 'selective serotonin reuptake inhibitors.' Normally, the body reabsorbs serotonin. SSRIs stop the body from reabsorbing serotonin, leaving higher levels of serotonin to circulate. A lack of serotonin has been shown to increase episodes of depression and violent behaviour.

The activated Soothe system brings feelings of connection, belonging, and happiness. The deactivated Soothe system leads to feelings of isolation, loneliness, and worthlessness.

Meditation activates the Soothe system and practices such as the loving-kindness meditation, which we introduce in this lesson, have been shown to increase production and circulation of both oxytocin and serotonin. Generosity comes from a place of compassion and fosters a sense of connection. The feeling of being part of and contributing to something bigger activates the Soothe system.

We need all three systems in balance. Unfortunately, many of us spend most of our time in either threat or drive. To paraphrase the neuroscientist Rick Hanson, to hardwire happiness we need to pet the lizard, feed the mouse, and hug the monkey.

Why Kindness is Good For You - And the Importance of Boundaries

There is a lot of scientific evidence to suggest that kindness has many health benefits. When we perform an act of kindness, or even witness an act of kindness, this can stimulate the production of oxytocin. Oxytocin is one of the hormones associated with the soothing and contentment system. An increase in oxytocin helps us to feel safer and more connected. Oxytocin can even help to relieve pain.

Kindness makes us happier. When we perform an act of kindness this can boost our self-esteem. We feel good about ourselves. A study from UC Berkeley Greater Good Science Center found that around half of their research participants felt that they had more energy after performing an act of kindness. Many of the research participants also reported a reduction in symptoms of anxiety and depression.

In order to be truly kind and generous towards others, we need to be aware of others. Maybe we are out shopping and spot something that we think a friend will like. Maybe we take the time to listen to a loved one who is struggling. In those moments our attention moves away from ourselves and our own worries and we connect with someone else. Our world becomes bigger and more connected.

When we are kind, this kindness is often met with gratitude and the acts of kindness are reciprocated. We don't give in order to receive but it is a pleasant by-product.

However, being generous does not mean being a martyr. Being generous does not mean self-sacrifice. We also need to recognise the importance of boundaries in relationships. When you are kind, does it feel like a moment of connection, or do you feel taken advantage of? Are you being kind because you want to or because you fear rejection if you don't?

Are you giving your time and energy to others to the detriment of yourself? Are you doing things for others that you are not comfortable doing or that you know that they could do for themselves? Sometimes the kindest thing we can do is set a boundary. In doing so we are being kind to ourselves and honest with others and saying no. Notice how it feels when you give. If you feel resentful, or burnt out, then it is not generous!

When we practice kindness and generosity this needs to include self-kindness. This is often the most difficult aspect of, kindness. The kindness meditation can help us to develop this skill.

Introduction to the Kindness Meditation

The kindness meditation is a practice that is designed to train the mind to develop positive thoughts and feelings towards ourselves and others. The practice is divided into five stages with a different focus in each stage. Throughout the practice, we are not forcing ourselves to feel anything different, but we are planting seeds of kindness. Many people find that they feel quite warm and positive when they practice this meditation. But whatever you feel is absolutely fine!

In the first stage we connect with ourselves. We notice what we appreciate about ourselves. We connect with our own innate value as a human being. And we see if we can meet ourselves with kindness. For many of us, self-kindness is quite an alien concept, so this is often the most difficult stage. However, we are not trying to force ourselves to feel something. Instead, we are setting an intention towards self-kindness. In time and with practice, this meditation can help us to be kinder to ourselves and to be less self-critical.

In the second stage we connect with a friend. This is someone who we have straightforward positive feelings towards. We imagine our friend. We reflect on what we like and appreciate about our friend. We connect with a sense of our shared humanity. We wish our friend well. And we notice how this feels.

In the third stage we direct our attention towards a neutral person. This is someone who we don't particularly like or dislike. It might be someone we don't know particularly well such as the postman or someone who works at the local shop. And we are doing the same thing as with stages one and two. We connect with what we appreciate - this might need a little imagination. We connect with a sense of our shared humanity. We connect with a sense of well-wishing. And we notice how this feels.

In the fourth stage we bring to mind someone that we find difficult in some way. When you are first learning this practice it is best to pick someone where the difficulty is quite mild. So if you have an enemy don't pick them just yet! We connect with what we appreciate - there is more to this person than the aspect we find difficult. We connect with a sense of our shared humanity. We connect with a sense of well-wishing. And we notice how this feels.

In the final stage we bring to mind all four people - ourselves, our friend, the neutral person and the person we find difficult, and we see if we can connect equally with all four. And then we open up to connect with as many people as possible.

Kindness to Self and a Friend

As we have just seen, the kindness meditation is traditionally a five-stage meditation. However, in this lesson we are going to focus on two stages - ourselves and our friend. For many of us self-kindness is the most difficult and kindness toward a friend is the easiest stage. For this practice we will begin with our friend and use our feelings towards our friend as a way in to being kind to ourselves.

- Find yourself a comfortable meditation posture. Lightly close your eyes if that feels comfortable for you. Connect with a sense of being grounded.
- Bring your attention to your breath. Notice the changing sensations of breathing. Letting go of the out-breath and welcoming in the next in-breath.
- When you are ready, bring to mind a friend. You might have an image of your friend, or a sense of them in some other way.
- Notice how it feels to think of your friend. Notice what you appreciate about them.
- Connect with all the things that you have in common. All the things that make us human. Your friend is breathing, just as you are. Your friend experiences pleasure and pain, joy and sorrow just as you do. Your friend has skills just as you do, and makes mistakes just as you do. These are all the things that make us human.
- See if you can wish your friend well. Imagine your friend smiling at you. Imagine that your friend is really happy.

Imagine saying to your friend. 'I wish you happiness. I wish you good health. I wish you peace.' Or whatever works for you.

- Notice how this feels. Notice how it feels to connect with your friend with kindness.
- Then imagine that your friend is doing this meditation. What might your friend appreciate about you? What qualities might your friend value in you?
- Imagine that your friend is smiling at you and wishing you well. Imagine your friend saying to you 'I wish you happiness. I wish you good health. I wish you peace.' Or whatever works for you.
- Notice how this feels.
- Finally, allow the image or the sense of your friend to fade away and connect back with a sense of yourself. See if you can appreciate yourself just for being human. See if you can wish yourself well. 'I wish myself happiness. I wish myself good health. I wish myself peace.' Or whatever works for you.
- When you are ready start to observe the sounds around you. Bring the meditation to a close and open your eyes when you are ready.

Summary

When we practice meditation, we pay attention to ourselves, and this is an act of generosity. When we broaden the definitions of kindness and generosity, we can start to use them interchangeably. When we are generous, we give - but this does not need to be material.

The memories of generosity meditation helps us to recognise moments when we have received, given and witnessed generosity. This probably happens more than we are aware of. The practice also reminds us of the interplay between gratitude and generosity. When we recognise and feel gratitude for the generosity we receive, this can give us a sense of abundance and make us more likely to be generous. It's like a really positive feedback loop!

The emotion regulation systems is a model developed by Professor Paul Gilbert. The Threat system concerns our response to perceived danger. An over-developed or over-stimulated threat system can lead to anxiety, and this can be managed by mindfulness meditation practice. The Drive system concerns our human need to achieve and acquire and can become quite addictive. The practice of gratitude can help to regulate the potential compulsive nature of the Drive system. Finally, the Soothe system concerns downregulation, connection and relaxation and is usually the system that is least developed. All mindfulness practice can help with this!

Kindness can be good for us in many ways. It helps us to feel connected to others; it gives us a sense of purpose and wellbeing. It can even reduce pain and reduce symptoms of depression and anxiety. However, we must be careful not to burnout. Sometimes saying no is the kindest - and most honest thing we can do! And it is also important to remember that kindness includes ourselves.

The kindness meditation is a practice in which we set an intention to cultivate a sense of kindness and well-wishing towards ourselves and others. In the practice we focus on ourselves, a friend, a neutral person, a challenging person and then open up to connect with the world.

Finally in this lesson we practised the first two stages of the kindness meditation. In this lesson we start with our friend and use our positive feelings towards our friend as a way in to being kind to ourselves. We focus on what we share rather than our differences and we remember that, just as we like our friend, our friend probably likes us too!

Home practice

This week see if you can practice a kindness to self and a friend meditation each day. Notice any thoughts and feelings that you experience. Remember that you are not trying to force yourself to feel a certain way. Also this week see if you can practice a memories of generosity meditation. You might choose to practice this as a formal meditation, or you might use your journal to write down examples of moments in which you have experienced generosity either as the giver, the receiver, or the witness. The more we do this the more we notice. You might even find that more opportunities to practice generosity appear and as you take those opportunities this generosity is reciprocated.

Questions for Reflection

Q1. Do you find that you are more likely to notice moments or giving or receiving?

Q2. Are there certain kinds of generosity that are easier to give or receive than others?

Q3. What gets in the way of practising generosity?

12

lesson Eight: patience

This lesson's attitude is patience. This does not mean passively waiting for things to happen but recognising that change takes time. We might need to put in some effort when learning a new skill but when we are impatient and expect instant results, we are more likely to give up. In this lesson we continue to explore the kindness meditation, this time in relation to a stranger, someone that we find challenging, and the whole world. You can see why patience might be helpful! We also introduce two practices to help us to gain a sense of perspective, recognising that no matter how difficult life might seem, there is always more to the story and there is always something to appreciate.

Home Practice Review - Why is Self-Kindness so Difficult?

Last lesson we introduced the kindness meditation and we practiced kindness towards ourselves and a friend. For many of us self-kindness is the most difficult part of the practice. Why is it so difficult to be kind to ourselves?

Unfortunately, many of us have had negative experiences in childhood in which we have been told that we are not good enough. Perhaps our parents were abusive or neglectful or not emotionally available. Even if our parents were doing their best, we might have picked up messages that we are not worthy of kindness. Alternatively, we may have been bullied at school and this unpleasant experience taught us not to be kind to ourselves.

We live in a world in which self-sacrifice is often celebrated but we are not always encouraged to be kind to ourselves. This can lead us to believe that self-kindness is selfish. Advertisers often tell us that self-care means spending lots of money on beauty products or candles, but *genuine* self-kindness can be more challenging. For many of us it is quite easy to find time to help someone else but then we find that we are too busy to take time out for ourselves

Many of us find it difficult and uncomfortable to take a compliment. And yet, when we receive an insult or a criticism, not only do we believe it, but we also dwell on it. In lesson three we looked at the concept of negativity bias. This is our tendency to overlook the positive and dwell on the negative. And we often do this when it comes to receiving feedback. Not only that but many of us are afraid that if we take a compliment or if we recognise our positive qualities then we might appear arrogant, and people might not like us.

Tips for Self-Kindness

As with everything we have looked at, self-kindness is a practice. Many of us are so used to listening to our own inner critic that listening to something positive can feel alien. However, one of the reasons why we are so comfortable with self-criticism is because it is so familiar. Our minds are lazy, and we think in particular ways simply because that is what we have always done. Every time we criticise ourselves it becomes easier to do so again.

This is where positive affirmations can be helpful. An affirmation is a positive statement that we can use to challenge the more negative self-talk. Some people find it helpful to state their affirmation three times in front of the mirror as soon as they get out of bed in the morning. This is also a way of setting an intention for the day. For example, if you want to learn to be more resilient you might say:

'I am resilient; I am resilient; I am resilient.' or if you have a harsh inner critic and a tendency towards perfectionism you might try saying:

'I am enough; I am enough; I am enough.'

Starting a regular practice of saying positive affirmations will probably feel really uncomfortable at first. But the more we do it, the easier it will become.

Self-kindness can be difficult when we compare ourselves with other people. When we do this, kindness becomes conditional. We tell ourselves that we need to achieve certain things before we are worthy of kindness. This is simply not true. When we start to practice self-kindness and self-compassion, we connect with all the things that we have in common with our fellow human beings. We connect with a sense of our shared humanity. When we remind ourselves of how much we share with others we can begin to treat ourselves with the same kindness and compassion that we would have for everyone else.

Remember when we are practising the kindness meditation, we are not trying to make anything happen. Sometimes we will feel pleasant emotions. We might feel a sense of warmth towards ourselves and others. But we might not. Whatever you feel is absolutely fine! When we practice the kindness meditation, we are setting an intention. Then we wait and see what happens.

Patience

"Patience is not passive waiting. Patience is active acceptance of the process required to attain your goals and dreams."
— **Ray A. Davis**

Growth and healing take time. They require patience and action. Any new skill requires practice and patience and over time what seemed difficult at first starts to become easier and after time automatic.

Patience is letting things unfold in their own time; persevering when nothing seems to be changing. Change happens in its own time. Rather than criticising our 'slow' progress, appreciate how far we have come and take pleasure in the journey.

A lack of patience can often be counter-productive, diminishing or even ruining the intended outcome. A cake takes time to bake. However tempting it may be, premature removal from the oven will probably lead to disappointment.

Practice patience with yourself. Why rush through some moments in order to reach other 'better' ones? Each one is your life in that moment.

Patience in Practice.

There are many activities that we can undertake to develop and practice patience. Activities such as gardening and baking are naturally patient. We plant the seeds, literally and metaphorically, and wait for something to emerge of its own accord. Poetry can also be a patient activity. You cannot skim read a poem. Instead, we take our time and allow the words to unfold. And nature teaches us about patience. Notice your response to the weather and the seasons. Are you desperately waiting for the spring to arrive? And spring to become summer? Can we patiently observe the first snowdrops without rushing to the next thing and the next?

Remind yourself that there is no need to be impatient with yourself because you find your mind judging all the time or because you are tense or agitated or frightened, or because you have been practicing mindfulness for some time and you are not noticing dramatic enough changes. To be patient is simply to be completely open to each moment, accepting it in its fullness, knowing that things can only unfold in their own time.

Mark's Story: The Impatient Rock Star

When I was a teenager, I dreamed of being a rock star. I wanted to be a lead guitarist, I had been told by too many people that I couldn't sing to believe I could be a lead singer. However, wanting to play guitar and being able to play, are separate things. I struggled with different chords, chord changes and trying to bring them together to produce a tune. I decided very quickly that the problem was too many strings. I exchanged my six string for a four string bass guitar, surely this would be easier. The number of strings was not the issue, it was my lack of patience. I never mastered the bass and never became a rock star. However, over the years I have developed a number of skills and realise that most things seem hard before they either become easy or we give up. The key factor to which option we decide upon is patience.

The Kindness Meditation: Kindness to a Neutral Person/ Stranger

In this stage we bring to mind someone that we neither like nor dislike. We connect with someone for whom we don't have strong feelings either way. And it doesn't matter if we don't know the person particularly well because we have so much in common with them as a fellow human being - and that's enough! And don't worry if you don't feel anything. We are not trying to make anything happen, but we are setting an intention towards kindness.

• Find yourself a comfortable meditation posture. Lightly

close your eyes if that feels comfortable for you. Connect with a sense of being grounded.

- Bring your attention to your breath. Notice the changing sensations of breathing. Letting go of the out-breath and welcoming in the next in-breath.

- When you are ready, bring to mind a neutral person. This might be a stranger that you know by sight but don't know very well - such as the person who works in your local shop, or someone who gets on the same bus as you each morning. You might have an image of this person, or a sense of them in some other way.

- Notice how it feels to think of this neutral person. Notice what you appreciate about them. You might need to use some imagination here. Or you might appreciate the job that they do. Perhaps you could think of your bus driver and appreciate the fact that they do this role – or even recall times when they have smiled at you whilst giving you your ticket. It doesn't need to be anything huge – just opening to the possibility to appreciation and connection.

- Connect with all the things that you have in common. All the things that make us human. This person is breathing, just as you are. This person experiences pleasure and pain, joy and sorrow, just as you do. This person has skills just as you do and makes mistakes just as you do. These are all the things that make us human.

- See if you can wish this stranger well. Imagine this neutral person smiling at you. Imagine that this person is really happy. Imagine saying to your neutral person. 'I wish you happiness. I wish you good health. I wish you peace.' Or whatever works for you.

- Notice how this feels. Notice how it feels to connect with a neutral person with kindness.
- When you are ready start to observe the sounds around you. Bring the meditation to a close and open your eyes when you are ready.

Kindness to a Challenging Person

In this stage we bring to mind someone that you find challenging in some way. Choose someone where the difficulty is quite mild, at least when you are first learning the practice. If you have an enemy, or there is someone in your life who has caused you significant distress you might want to wait until you are more familiar with this practice before bringing them to mind. However, you might never want to bring kindness to that person and that's ok too.

Remember, whoever we choose, we are not trying to like the person, we are just connecting with them as a fellow human being.

- Find yourself a comfortable meditation posture. Lightly close your eyes if that feels comfortable for you. Connect with a sense of being grounded.
- Bring your attention to your breath. Notice the changing sensations of breathing. Letting go of the out-breath and welcoming in the next in-breath.
- When you are ready, bring to mind someone that you

find difficult or challenging. You might have an image of this person, or a sense of them in some other way.

- Notice how it feels to think of this challenging person. Notice what you appreciate about them. Perhaps there is more to this person than the aspect you don't like!

- Connect with all the things that you have in common. All the things that make us human. This person is breathing, just as you are. This person experiences pleasure and pain, joy and sorrow, just as you do. This person has skills just as you do and makes mistakes just as you do. These are all the things that make us human.

- See if you can wish this challenging person well. You are not condoning their behaviour or learning to like this person. Instead, you are connecting with a sense of well-wishing. Imagine this person that you find difficult smiling at you. Imagine that this person is really happy. Imagine saying to your challenging person. 'I wish you happiness. I wish you good health. I wish you peace.' Or whatever works for you.

- Notice how this feels. Notice how it feels to connect with someone who you find difficult and meeting them with kindness.

- When you are ready start to observe the sounds around you. Bring the meditation to a close and open your eyes when you are ready.

Kindness to the World

In this stage we bring to mind all four people - ourselves, our friend, the neutral person and the person we find challenging.

We see if we can connect equally with all four people. As with all the stages you are not trying to force yourself to feel a particular way, but you are setting an intention to develop kindness and connection. We then extend this to include more and more people.

- Find yourself a comfortable meditation posture. Lightly close your eyes if that feels comfortable for you. Connect with a sense of being grounded.
- Bring your attention to your breath. Just notice the changing sensations of breathing. Letting go of the out-breath and welcoming in the next in-breath.
- When you are ready, bring to mind all four people from the previous stages. You might imagine that you are sitting in a room with your friend, the neutral person and the person you find challenging. Notice how it feels to connect with all four people. See if you can connect with all the things that you have in common - all the things that make you human.
- You might imagine that all four people are smiling. You might try saying to yourself. 'I wish us happiness. I wish us good health. I wish us peace.' Or whatever works for you.
- When you are ready see if you can bring to mind more people. You might imagine the people in your street, the people in your town, around the country and around the world. You might imagine connecting with people you know and people that you don't know. You might imagine connecting with a range of people from different walks of life.

- See if you can connect with all the things that we have in common - all the things that make us human.
- You might imagine that you are all smiling. You might try saying to yourself. 'I wish us all happiness. I wish us all good health. I wish us all peace.' Or whatever works for you.
- You might imagine that a light is extending from your heart around the world.
- Notice how it feels to connect with the world.
- When you are ready start to observe the sounds around you. Bring the meditation to a close and open your eyes when you are ready.

Perspective Exercise: Putting a 'Bad Day' in Perspective

At the end of a day, it is easy to focus on all the things that went wrong. Maybe only one thing went wrong but that is taking all of our attention. This exercise can help. To do this exercise you will need an a4 piece of paper and a pen. You might choose to do this exercise at the end of the day as you reflect on how your day went.

Step one

- Draw a sad face in the middle of your piece of paper. This doesn't need to be artistic. The face should be around 2 inches or 5 cm in diameter.
- Next to the sad face, write one difficult thing that has happened that day - Don't pick anything huge. Maybe pick something that you have found irritating.

- Notice how you feel when you look at the sad face. Remember, there is no right or wrong way to feel.

Step two

- Next, draw five smiley faces around the outside of the paper, of equal size to the sad face, or slightly bigger.
- Next to each smiley face, write one thing that you have appreciated that day. For example. 'the traffic was quieter than usual on the way home,' 'the nights are getting lighter,' 'my colleague was really supportive when I told her about the situation above'... Make sure you come up with at least five positives!
- look at your paper now and notice if you feel any different.
- What is important is that we are not trying to make the difficult - sad face - go away. But we are putting it in perspective. this exercise can also be used when a friend or loved one has irritated us in some way. In step one you might draw a sad face and write down how this person has irritated you and in step two you might come up with five things that you appreciate about that person. Notice if that changes the way you feel about the situation.

The Bigger Container Meditation

In the bigger container meditation, we develop a sense of perspective in the present moment by noticing both pleasant and unpleasant experiences. We begin by allowing ourselves to turn towards whatever is unpleasant in the present moment, such as a physical pain or a difficult emotion. We then turn our attention towards something pleasant in the present moment. This might be the feeling of being warm enough, or the sensations of breathing. We then see if we can be aware of the pleasant and the unpleasant at the same time. This practice is a reminder that no matter how difficult things are, there is always something pleasant. By putting our unpleasant experiences into a bigger container of awareness we might not be able to get rid of the unpleasant experiences, but we are able to cope with them more effectively.

- Find yourself a comfortable meditation posture. Lightly close your eyes if that feels comfortable for you. Connect with a sense of being grounded.
- Bring your attention to your breath. Just notice the changing sensations of breathing. Letting go of the out-breath and welcoming in the next in-breath.
- When you are ready turn your attention towards something in your present moment experience that is unpleasant. This might be a physical sensation or an emotion. See if you can observe the experience with a sense of interest and curiosity. You are not trying to fix or change anything. You are simply observing.

- If you can't find anything unpleasant that's absolutely fine. Please don't search for unpleasant experiences!
- Next, when you are ready, turn your attention towards something in your present moment that is pleasant. Remember there is *always* something pleasant. It doesn't need to be anything huge. You might notice and appreciate your breath, or you might notice feeling warm and comfortable. You might notice a pleasant sound. Or you might open your eyes and notice something beautiful you can see around you. Whatever it is see if you can appreciate whatever is pleasant about this present moment.
- When you are ready broaden out your attention so that you are aware of both the pleasant and the unpleasant at the same time. What else can you be aware of?
- In your own time bring the meditation to a close and open your eyes when you are ready.

Summary

When we practice patience, we recognise that things take time. It takes time to learn a new skill such as a musical instrument of the art of meditation. It can also take time to notice the effects of our mindfulness practice. When we are patient, we can notice how far we have come rather than lamenting how far we have yet to go.

When we practice kindness towards a stranger and towards someone we find challenging, this provides us with an opportunity to practice patience. We may need to be patient with ourselves as we might not always feel the emotions that we would like to feel as we meditate. We may need to be patient with others as we bring to mind someone who has upset or irritated us in some way.

The perspective exercise is a reminder that our lives are generally a mixture of pleasant and unpleasant experiences. When we focus on the negative this can feel overwhelming and it can intensify unpleasant emotions. However, when we put our negative experiences into perspective, we can find that our difficulties are more manageable.

Although we tend to focus on the negative or on our painful experiences, in any moment there is always something to appreciate it - we just need to look for it!

Home Practice

This week see if you can practice a kindness meditation each day. You might choose kindness to a stranger, kindness to a difficult person, or kindness to the world. Or you might choose to combine the stages. Notice any thoughts and feelings that you experience. Remember that you are not trying to force yourself to feel a certain way. Also, this week see if you can practice a perspective exercise. This is particularly helpful if you feel that you have had a bad day. You might also take up an activity that helps you to practice patience such as baking, gardening, or reading poetry. Make a note of any observations in your journal.

Questions for Reflection:

Q1. What does impatience feel like?

Q2. In what situations are you more likely to be impatient? Are you more impatient with yourself, with others or with situations?

Q3. How does it feel to be kind to someone you find challenging?

13

lesson nine: trust

This is the last lesson of the course. We really hope that you have enjoyed reading this book and practising with us as much as we have enjoyed creating the course. In this final lesson we will be exploring the attitude of trust, in relation to ourselves, others and our mindfulness practice. We will also be taking the opportunity to summarise the learning of the previous nine lessons and finally offer a definition of what mindfulness actually is!

In this lesson we will also be introducing two simple bitesize practices. These are the head, heart, gut meditation, and the centring exercise. The head, heart, gut exercise is a useful meditation to enable us to connect with our thoughts, our values, and our intuition in relation to a question or dilemma. The centring exercise is an important practice in reminding us of our strength, standing and status and can help with confidence building.

Finally, we explore the next steps - how to take your mindfulness practice forward into a mindful future.

Home Practice Review: Kindness Practice Challenges

In lesson eight we introduced the attitude of patience and we practised three stages of the kindness meditation. We practised kindness to a stranger or a neutral person. We practiced kindness towards someone we find difficult or challenging. And we practised kindness towards the world. Challenges might come up in all of these stages.

When practising kindness towards a neutral person you might find that you don't have a strong emotional response. You might even feel bored. This is absolutely fine. Please do not criticise yourself for this. Instead, see if you can be interested in the boredom. What is it like to be bored? Where do you feel that boredom in the body? Often when we become interested in boredom we cease to be bored! Often patience and curiosity can be an antidote to boredom. Once we look at boredom without trying to fight it, it transforms of its own accord.

Sometimes when practising kindness towards someone you find challenging you might feel anger or resentment toward this person. This might be because you chose someone who was too challenging. Maybe the hurt is too recent or too raw. Perhaps if you have just gone through a break-up, for example, it might be wise to wait a while before bringing your ex to mind in a kindness practice. However, it is ok to feel anger. Anger is a healthy emotion that helps to keep us safe. However, we can sometimes become stuck in our anger, and this can be distressing.

Remember, we are not trying to feel anything in particular. We are starting from where we are and planting seeds of kindness. We are also not trying to like this challenging person and we are certainly not condoning inappropriate behaviour. Instead, we are connecting with this person's humanity and opening up to the possibility that we can let go of resentment. And when we let go of resentment towards someone who has hurt us in some way, we are not doing it because they deserve our forgiveness. We are doing it because we deserve peace. And when we connect with kindness towards a difficult person this does not mean letting go of our boundaries. We can have a sense of kindness from a distance without welcoming a toxic person back into our lives.

When we connect with kindness towards the world this might feel overwhelming. Perhaps you have certain political views that make it difficult to connect with people with opposing views. Perhaps you are aware of people who commit acts of cruelty around the world. Perhaps you could spend some time looking for positive news stories to remind yourself of the good in the world. Perhaps you could connect with the idea that people often do horrible things because they are suffering, and that kindness doesn't mean condoning this behaviour. And perhaps you could start small - you might start by bringing a sense of kindness to your street or town and build up from there!

Trust

Trust is earned in the smallest of moments. It is earned not through heroic deeds, or even highly visible actions, but through paying attention, listening, and gestures of genuine care and connection.

Brene Brown

For many of us trust can be difficult. Maybe we have had experiences in which we have felt let down or taken advantage of and this has made us wary of others. Perhaps we have been told that we are wrong so many times that we no longer trust our own judgement. Or perhaps we have picked up from our parents or the media that it is foolish and naive to be trusting and that a healthy dose of cynicism will keep us safe.

However, we must trust all the time in order to live our lives. We are constantly relying on others even when we don't realise it. When we make ourselves a cup of tea, we need to trust that the water is safe to drink and that we won't be electrocuted by the kettle! Although there are no guarantees in life, we need a basic level of trust in order to function. For example, while there are sometimes accidents on the roads, we need to trust that other drivers are competent and wish to drive safely, otherwise we wouldn't be able to get behind the wheel!

Trust is not the same as blind faith. We trust because we have evidence to support that trust. For example, you have been practising mindfulness for the last eight weeks and hopefully you have noticed some positive effects, and this is helping you to gain trust in the practices and your own ability to put your learning into action. For some people it is also helpful to look at the increasing scientific evidence supporting the benefits of mindfulness.

When we trust in others, we do so with the knowledge that they will let us down. As human beings we are imperfect, and we make mistakes. As we get to know ourselves, we learn that we ultimately have our own best interests at heart - even when we sabotage ourselves, we are ultimately trying to keep ourselves safe. As we get to know ourselves better, we can learn to rely on our intuition more. Trust takes time and practice. We need to find people who deserve our trust, and we need to practice listening to ourselves.

When we let go of doubt and learn to trust we can live more wholeheartedly. We cannot protect ourselves from disappointment, but we can live more connected lives.

What Mindfulness Is

Intentionally, we have resisted the temptation to provide definitions and explanations of what mindfulness is. There are a plethora of definitions and interpretations of what mindfulness is. Our intention has been to allow you, the listener, to develop your own definition and understanding of the processes and principles of mindfulness.

However, here are some of the more commonly used definitions:

Mindfulness is awareness that arises through paying attention, on purpose, in the present moment, non-judgementally," says Jon Kabat-Zinn. *"And then I sometimes add, in the service of self-understanding and wisdom."*

'Mindfulness is deliberately paying attention to our moment-by-moment experience, with an attitude of friendliness and curiosity.'

Mason-John and Groves, 2014

"Mindfulness is a state of awareness that enables us to make better choices about how we respond to our experiences even in difficult circumstances.'

www.breathworksmindfulness.org.uk

As we have explored the foundational attitudes, we can build up a more detailed understanding of what mindfulness actually is and what it means to live a mindful life.

As stated in the introduction, mindfulness starts with an intention. An intention to be aware in the present moment and to apply the foundational attitudes. It is not enough to simply practice mindfulness, we need to know why we are doing it. Otherwise we are simply going through the motions.

As we discovered in lesson one, mindfulness involves bringing a sense of curiosity to our experience - or beginner's mind. We can bring this beginners mind to any activity - and often the simpler the better.

In lesson two we explored the attitude of non-judgement. This is an important reminder that there is no right or wrong way to experience our mindfulness practice. It is important that we set aside time to practice but what happens during that practice is often beyond our control. What we feel is what we feel! Nothing to fix, nothing to change, nothing to judge. Doesn't that take the pressure off? This is particularly useful when practising a body scan meditation. Can you observe the felt sensations of your body just as it is without becoming caught up in judgement?

As we discovered in lesson three, mindfulness is not a robotic, emotionless detached awareness. Instead, we bring a sense of gratitude to our practice and our lives. We might practice gratitude in a formal meditation or through reflection or writing. And the more we practise gratitude, the more we notice things to be grateful for!

In lesson four we introduced the idea of acceptance. This

does not mean passively putting up with situations that we can change but it means that we no longer fight reality. In many ways this is the hardest attitude to fully understand. And yet when we begin to put it into action, we can experience greater freedom.

In lesson five we considered how much effort we should make in meditation and in life. Non-striving or balanced effort serves as a reminder not to try too hard but at the same time not to give up. In the mindfulness of breathing meditation, we learn to manage thoughts without striving to focus. When we practice meditation, we actively choose to focus on the object of concentration - such as the breath. However, we cannot force ourselves to feel a particular way. This is a common theme throughout the course because it is so important. What we feel is what we feel!

In lesson six we introduced the concept of letting go. As we tune into our moment-by-moment experience, we notice how everything constantly changes. We let go of one moment to welcome in the next. We notice this breath in the moment, without clinging onto the breath that has passed. We notice our experience now, not our ideas about our experience in the future.

Mindfulness might also be defined as heartfulness. In lesson seven we introduced the kindness meditation and the attitude of generosity. Mindfulness is not a solitary navel gazing practice. Instead, it teaches us to connect with others.

And in week eight we were reminded that this can often take patience. We don't always like everyone and that is ok. But we can choose to connect with their humanity. This is not always easy and might not always feel pleasant but practicing with patience means welcoming in all of our experience and allowing it to unfold in its own time.

Taking all of our learning into account we would define mindfulness as:

A radical and courageous practice in becoming aware of ourselves and our experiences in the present moment in order that we can live our lives more wholeheartedly.

Rachel

Or

Knowing what is happening now in order to live a life on purpose

Mark

Head-Heart-Gut Meditation: Listening to Your Intuition to Make Mindful Decisions

The following is an adaptation of a practice developed by Google's 'Search Inside Yourself' leadership development programme.

The head, heart, gut meditation is particularly useful when we have an important decision to make. By bringing in our cognition, our values, and our intuition, we can make more wholehearted decisions. This can also be helpful in our reflective practice. You may choose to use this meditation when reflecting on any of the questions that have been asked of you during the course so far.

Perhaps your answers are different when you bring your whole self into your response.

Grounding

- Find a posture that feels comfortable for you. You may

choose to sit on a chair or you may choose to sit on a cushion on the floor. You may choose to lie down on a mat or on your bed. You may choose to do the practice standing up. It is entirely up to you.

- You might find it helpful to close your eyes. This is entirely up to you.
- Soften any tension that you might be holding.
- Ground yourself in whatever way feels right for you. You may bring your attention to your breath or to the sensations of contact with your chair or support.

When you are ready, bring to mind a question or a dilemma that you are working with.

Head

- Bring the question or dilemma to mind and see if you can observe any thoughts or images that emerge as you do so.
- See if you can observe and take note of the thoughts without getting too involved. Not clinging on to the thoughts. You do not need to analyse the thoughts or actively engage with them. Instead, see if you can observe the thoughts that arise as you ask yourself the question. So you are simply observing what's here in this moment.

What do I think about this issue?

Heart

- See if you can connect with your values. You might place

one hand on your heart and ask yourself what is truly important right now.

- You might become aware of an emotion, or an image. Remember there is no right or wrong - just notice what emerges for you. See if you can connect with your values; connect with what matters to you; connect with what you care about;
- Ask yourself the question again and notice any emotional response. What are your values in relation to the question?
- What is your intention in relation to the question?

What do I feel emotionally about this issue?

Gut

- Turn your attention to felt sensations in the body, particularly noticing the abdomen. Sensations may be subtle or might be more distinct. Just notice how it is for you when you bring this dilemma to mind.
- Tune into any intuition. Tune into what your body is telling you around the gut area - regarding this question.

What is my intuition about this issue?'

Gathering

- See if you can broaden your awareness to connect with your thinking, your values, and your body at the same time. You might also use your breath as an anchor. You might simply pause and see what emerges next.

- You might notice a deeper answer emerging from the question.

What shall I do now?
Ending

- When you are ready, come back to a sense of being grounded in the body.
- Observe the sounds around you.
- And letting go of any effort, bring the practice to a close, and open your eyes.

Centring Exercise

This practice is particularly helpful when you are experiencing self-doubt and need to inject some confidence. It uses the metaphor of a tree. It is a reminder of your roots - everything that got you to where you are today. And it is a reminder of your presence and your influence on the world. It combines posture and visualisation. Ideally the practice is done standing but you can adapt it so that it is comfortable for you.

Beginning

- Find yourself a comfortable standing or sitting position where you can have a sense of being grounded. If you are standing, stand with your feet hip distance apart. If you are sitting, then see if you can sit with your feet flat on the floor.
- You might choose to close your eyes. This is entirely up to you.

Roots

- Bring your attention to the soles of your feet. Notice the contact of the feet on the floor.
- When you are ready, imagine roots extending from your feet into the ground, extending down and to each side and forward and back.
- These roots represent all that got you to where you are today, all the learning and self-development over the years, your training and education, all those supporting you - loved ones, work colleagues, friends, people who inspire you.
- Notice how grounded and supported you feel. Take a few deep breaths, connecting with your roots.

Trunk

- Imagine a thread pulling you gently skywards from the crown of your head. Roll your shoulders back and down.
- You might imagine your body as being like the trunk of a tree.
- Allow a sense of your presence, your dignity, and your right to be here in this world. You might have a sense of the strength of a tree.
- Notice how tall and strong you feel. Take a few deep breaths, connecting with your trunk.

Branches

- When you are ready, raise your arms out to the sides and stretch your fingers outwards.
- You might imagine your arm and fingers as the branches of a tree.
- Reflect on the impact you have in the world. The support you offer to friends and loved ones; the difference you make in your work, hobbies or volunteering. You might recall the last time you were kind or friendly to someone or a time when you made someone laugh.
- Notice how wide you feel. Take a few deep breaths, connecting with your branches.

Closing

- Bring your arms back down to your sides. Take a few moments to tune into what matters to you, what you really care about, what you value most.
- Take a couple of deep breaths. When you are ready, bring the practice to a close.

Our Practice Challenges:

Mark's Story: Maintaining Authenticity

The biggest challenge I have faced, and occasionally continue to face despite co-creating this course is maintaining authenticity. For most of my life I meditated in secret, very few people knew that I had a meditation practice. I was concerned that people would think it was some 'hippy nonsense.' Even after 'coming out' and training as a mindfulness trainer and now running a mindfulness business I notice an occasional reluctance in social settings to discuss my work in any depth. As mindfulness has become more mainstream, this has reduced along with the fear of ridicule.

However, to this day there are members of my family and friendship groups that do not understand what I do as a mindfulness trainer or practitioner. There are business people at networking meetings that see it as something people with problems do. There are still many people I meet who have not heard of or understand what it is. The constant need to explain and justify my practice sometimes results in self-doubt. If others don't do it or see the benefit, then am I deluding myself? My logical mind says that there are thousands of research papers to demonstrate the benefits and my gut tells me that it has helped me face countless challenges in my life. However, when I practice with others, when I spend time with other practitioners and teachers, my heart tells me that it is ok to be true to myself and my practice.

Rachel's Story: Practising Through Trauma

In 2019 I had a traumatic bereavement. In the weeks and months that followed I found that every time I sat down to meditate, I would be flooded with painful thoughts, memories, and emotions. This was overwhelming and incredibly distressing. As a mindfulness teacher I found it particularly upsetting that I was no longer able to find peace in meditation. In fact, I started to become frightened to meditate. I would happily lead meditation but the thought of being with my own thoughts and feelings terrified me.

However, in retrospect this was not surprising. Mindfulness is recognised as helpful in many situations and has been shown to help with chronic pain, chronic depression, stress and anxiety and many other difficulties. However, it is not recommended when someone's difficulties are acute. In 2019 my grief and trauma symptoms were acute not chronic, and meditation did not help.

During this time, I continued to have a mindfulness practice. However, instead of formally meditating, I would keep a gratitude journal or read poetry. I practised the attitudes of mindfulness through creative pursuits such as painting and playing the saxophone.

Grief never goes away. However, with time and therapy I was able to process the trauma. I returned to meditation. Initially I practised for five minutes at a time to see what would happen. It was like coming home. My mind is not always a delightful place to be but it no longer frightens me. It was like reuniting with an old friend - an old friend who didn't judge me for being away for so long.

The future - a Mindful Life...

Maintaining a Mindfulness Practice

You have now been practising mindfulness for around eight weeks. In week two we explored how we might begin a mindfulness practice and what this might be like. Many of the same points still apply but hopefully you know have a deeper understanding of what mindfulness is and why you wish to maintain your practice. The following tips may also help:

1. **Intention-Setting:** Take a moment now to reflect on your intentions for developing a mindfulness practice. You might choose to do this as a formal intention-setting meditation.

- Why did you embark on this mindfulness journey?

- What have you learned?
- Have you changed as you have begun to practice mindfulness?
- What is your intention for the future?

Hopefully as you reflect on these questions you will feel motivated to continue in your mindfulness practice.

1. **Reading, Reflecting and Journaling:** Throughout the course we have suggested that you reflect on your experiences and on specific questions and write your reflections in a journal. As we reach the end of the course, this might be an appropriate time to read back over what you have written. You might find it helpful to read other books about mindfulness and compassion. Or you might choose to watch online videos or listen to podcasts relating to mindfulness and gain inspiration from others. Of course, you can also read back over this book again and again. Many people find that repetition is incredibly beneficial in embedding an idea or practice. And if you read with beginner's mind, you might find that you notice different things each time you listen or that your understanding deepens.

2. **Applying the Attitudes:** We suggested that you meditate every day. If you did then that's great. However, if you missed a day, how did that feel? Can you apply the attitudes to the development of your practice? If you miss a day can you notice what that was like with curiosity and beginners mind rather than self-judgement? You might

notice whether you are more likely to practice when you are stressed and feel that you need it or on days when you are feeling relaxed. Can you treat your meditation practice as an act of generosity towards yourself rather than a chore or something to strive to achieve? How might you apply the other attitudes to your meditation practice?

3. **Seeking Support:** Maintaining a mindfulness practice means developing a new habit. This takes time. And it can be difficult to do alone. You might find it helpful to find a mindfulness group, either online or in your local area. Alternatively, you might buddy up with a friend so you can support one another. Why not give your friend a copy of this book so you can practice together?

4. **Mindful Reminders:** Mindfulness is simple but not easy but often the most difficult part is remembering to do it. You might set an alarm on your phone or add it to your to-do list. You might write a reminder on a post-it note on your fridge to remind yourself about mindful eating. You might write a reminder on a post-it note near your shoe-rack to remind yourself about mindful walking. The possibilities are endless and you can have fun with it!

5. **Keep it Simple:** Set a manageable goal. Often, we set ourselves up to fail by setting goals that are unachievable. Instead of deciding to meditate for 20 minutes every day, you might decide to do a bitesize practice 5 out of 7 days. Celebrate what you are doing rather than beating yourself up for what you are not.

Ending

We really hope you have enjoyed this book. Creating this course has been a really valuable experience for us as it has provided us with the opportunity to reflect on our own mindfulness practice. For both of us, our mindfulness and meditation practices have changed and developed over time as has our understanding of what it means to live a mindful life. Living a mindful life does not mean that life will suddenly become easy. However, it does mean that we are able to manage life's challenges with more resilience. When we live life more mindfully, we are able to live fuller, richer lives, appreciating the pleasant aspects of our experience and accepting the unpleasant. We are able to make choices about how to respond to life's difficulties. When we live more mindfully we live more connected lives, recognising all that we share with others. We would like to end this course with one of our favourite meditations.

Just Like Me Meditation

What follows is an adaptation of a practice by meditation trainer Ram Das. For this meditation you can bring to mind either a friend, stranger, neutral person or a group of people, it can be useful to use a photograph or image from the internet if you are comfortable practicing with your eyes open.

Grounding

- Find a posture that feels comfortable for you. You may choose to sit on a chair or you may choose to sit on a cushion on the floor. You may choose to lie down on a mat or on your bed. You may choose to do the practice standing up. It is entirely up to you.

- You might find it helpful to close your eyes. This is entirely up to you.
- Soften any tension that you might be holding.
- Ground yourself in whatever way feels right for you. You may bring your attention to your breath or to the sensations of contact with your chair or support.

Looking

- When you are ready, bring to mind an image of the person who you would like to connect with.
- Alternatively you can keep your eyes open and look at an image.

Phrases

Repeat the following phrases. This can either be silently, in your head, or out loud:

This person has a body and a mind, just like me.

This person came into this world as a vulnerable and helpless baby just like me

This person has feelings, emotions, and thoughts, just like me.

This person experienced love just like me

This person has experienced heartbreak just like me

This person has experienced physical and emotional pain and suffering, just like me.

This person has at some time been sad, disappointed, angry, or hurt, just like me.

This person has felt unworthy or inadequate, just like me.

This person has felt alone just like me

This person wants to belong just like me

This person has felt doubt and uncertainty just like me

This person worries and is frightened sometimes, just like me.

This person makes mistakes just like me

This person wants to be trusted, just like me.

This person has longed for friendship, just like me.

This person is learning about life, just like me.

This person is living through a pandemic just like me

This person wants to be caring and kind to others, just like me.

This person wants to be content with what life has given them, just like me.

This person wishes to be free from pain and suffering, just like me.

This person wishes to be safe and healthy, just like me.

This person wishes to be happy, just like me.

This person wishes to be loved, just like me.

Now, allow wishes for well-being to arise:

I wish this person to have the strength, resources, and social support they need to navigate the difficulties in life.

I wish this person to be free from pain and suffering.

I wish this person to be peaceful and happy.

I wish this person to be loved . . . because this person is a fellow human being, just like me.

Closing

• Bring the practice to a close whenever you are ready.

14

Guided Audio Meditations

All 19 guided meditations available via registration at

mindfultherapies.org.uk/registration

15

references and further reading

Juliet Adams (2016) *Mindful Leadership For Dummies*

Juliet Adams (2020) *Intention Matters: The science of creating the life you want*

Brene Brown (2015) *Daring Greatly: How the Courage to Be Vulnerable Transforms the Way We Live, Love, Parent and Lead*

Brene Brown (2018) *The Gifts Of Imperfection: Let Go of Who You Think You're Supposed to Be and Embrace Who You Are*

Vidyamala Burch, (2008)) ***Living Well with Pain and Illness: Using mindfulness to free yourself from suffering***

Vidyamala Burch and Danny Penman, (2013) ***Mindfulness for Health: A practical guide to relieving pain, reducing stress and restoring wellbeing***

Choden and Heather Regan-Addis (2018) *Mindfulness Based*

Living Course: A Self-Help Version of the Popular Mindfulness Eight-Week Course

Paul Gilbert (2010) **The Compassionate Mind**

Thich Nhat Hanh (2008) *The Miracle Of Mindfulness: The Classic Guide to Meditation by the World's Most Revered Master*

David R. Hamilton (2010) *Why Kindness is Good For You*

Rick Hanson (2014) *Hardwiring Happiness: How to reshape your brain and your life*

Tristen Inagaki and Lauren Ross (2018). 'Neural Correlates of Giving Social Support: Differences Between Giving Targeted Versus Untargeted Support.' *Psychosom Med.* 2018 Oct;80(8):724-732

Jon Kabat-Zinn (2004) *Wherever You Go, There You Are: Mindfulness Meditation for Everyday Life*

Jon Kabat-Zinn (2013) *Full Catastrophe Living, Revised Edition: How to cope with stress, pain and illness using mindfulness meditation.*

Jiddu Krishnamurti (1970) *Can the Mind Observe Without Comparison: Eight Small Group Discussions, Malibu, USA, (audio-book)*

Jiddu Krishnamurti (2019)) **Can The Mind Be Quiet?: Living, Learning and Meditation**

Kristin Neff (2011) *Self compassion*

Kristin Neff (2021) *Fierce Self-Compassion: How Women Can Harness Kindness to Speak Up, Claim Their Power, and Thrive*

Kristin Neff and Christopher Germer (2018) **The Mindful Self-Compassion Workbook: A Proven Way to Accept Yourself, Build Inner Strength, and Thrive**

Shunryu Suzuki (1973) *Zen Mind, Beginner's Mind*

Lau Tzu (2000) *Tao Te Ching*

Alan Watts (2009) *The Book: On the Taboo Against Knowing Who You Are*

Mark Williams and Danny Penman (2011) *Mindfulness: A Practical Guide to Finding Peace in a Frantic World*

thank you